Thought
Power

Thought Power

Its control and culture

By ANNIE BESANT

This publication made possible with the assistance of the Kern Foundation

The Theosophical Publishing House Wheaton, Illinois, U.S.A.
Madras, India/London, Eng.

Sixth Quest Book Printing, 1988. Published by The Theosophical Publishing House, a department of The Theosophical Society in America.

Library of Congress Cataloging in Publication data.

Besant, Annie (Wood) 1847-1933.
  Thought power, its control and culture.

  (Theosophical classics series)   (A Quest book)
  1. Thought and thinking.   2. Theosophy.
I. Title.
[BF455.B376   1973]   153   73-7644
ISBN 0-8356-0312-1

Printed in the United States of America

QUEST BOOKS
are published by The
Theosophical Society in
America, a branch of a
world organization
dedicated to the
promotion of
brotherhood and the
encouragement of the
study of religion,
philosophy, and
science, to the end
that man may better
understand himself and
his place in the universe.

Cover Illustration by
JANE EVANS

PUBLISHER'S NOTE

This book, first published in 1903, has continued to be in demand and has gone through numerous editions and reprintings. It has been slightly abridged for this Quest edition; a very few passages which are not relevant today have been eliminated, but this does not affect the main thesis in any way. Otherwise, except for minor editorial corrections, the book appears in the same form as when it was first published. The attention of the reader is called to the fact that certain terms such as *Ego, atom, ether,* and derivatives of these words, have a specialized meaning in theosophical literature and are therefore not to be regarded in the modern scientific sense.

CONTENTS

CONTENTS

FOREWORD

THIS little book is intended to help the student to study his own nature, so far as its intellectual part is concerned. If he masters the principles herein laid down, he will be in a fair way to co-operate with Nature in his own evolution, and to increase his mental stature far more rapidly than is possible while he remains ignorant of the conditions of his growth.

The Introduction may offer some difficulties to the lay reader, and may perhaps be skipped by such at the first reading. It is necessary, however, as a foundation for those who would see the relation of the intellect to the other parts of their nature and to the outer world. And those who would fulfill the maxim, "Know thyself," must not shrink from a little mental exertion, nor must expect mental food to drop ready-cooked from the sky into a lazily-opened mouth.

If the booklet helps even a few earnest students, and clears some difficulties out of the way, its purpose will have been served.

ANNIE BESANT

INTRODUCTION

THE value of knowledge is tested by its power to purify and ennoble the life, and all earnest students desire to apply the theoretical knowledge acquired in their study of Theosophy to the evolution of their own character and to the helping of their fellow-men. It is for such students that is written this little book, with the hope that a better understanding of their own intellectual nature may lead to a purposeful cultivation of what is good in it and an eradication of what is evil. The emotion which impels to righteous living is half wasted if the clear light of the intellect does not illuminate the path of conduct; for as the blind man strays from the way unknowing till he falls into the ditch, so does the Ego, blinded by ignorance, turn aside from the road of right living till he falls into the pit of evil action. Truly is Avidya—the privation of knowledge—the first step out of unity into separateness, and only as it lessens does separateness diminish, until its disappearance restores the Eternal Peace.

THE SELF AS KNOWER

In studying the nature of man, we separate the Man from the vehicles which he uses, the living Self from the garments with which he is clothed. The Self is one, however varying may be the forms of his manifestation, when working through and by means of the different kinds of matter. It is, of course, true that there is but One Self in the fullest sense of the words; that as rays flame forth from the sun, the Selves that are the true Men are but rays of the Supreme Self, and that each Self may whisper: "I am He." But for our present purpose, taking a single ray, we may assert also in its separation its own inherent unity, even though this be hidden by its forms. Consciousness is a unit, and the divisions we make in it are either made for purposes of study, or are illusions, due to the limitation of our perceptive power by the organs through which it works in the lower worlds. The fact that the manifestations of the Self proceed severally from his three aspects of knowing, willing, and energising —from which arise severally thoughts, desires, and actions—must not blind us to the other fact that there is no division of substance; the whole Self knows, the whole Self wills, the whole Self acts. Nor are the functions wholly separated; when he knows, he also acts and wills; when he acts, he also knows and wills; when he wills, he also acts and knows. One function is predominant, and sometimes to such an extent as to wholly veil the others; but even in the intensest concentration of knowing—the most separate of the three—there is always present a latent energising and a latent willing, discernible as present by careful analysis.

We have called these three "the three aspects of the Self"; a little further explanation may help towards understanding. When the Self is still, then is manifested the aspect of Knowledge, capable of taking on the likeness of any object presented. When the Self is concentrated, intent on change of state, then appears the aspect of Will. When the Self, in presence of any object, puts forth energy to contact that object, then shows forth the aspect of Action. It will thus be seen that these three are not separate divisions of the Self, not three things joined into one or compounded, but that there is one indivisible whole, manifesting in three ways.

It is not easy to clarify the fundamental conception of the Self further than by his mere naming. The Self is that conscious, feeling, ever-existing One, that in each of us knows himself as existing. No man can ever think of himself as non-existent, or formulate himself to himself in consciousness as "I am not." As Bhagavan Das has put it: "The Self is the indispensable first basis of life. . . . In the words of Vachaspati-Mishra, in his Commentary (the *Bhamati*) on the *Shariraka-Bhashya* of Sankaracharya: 'No one doubts "Am I?" or "Am I not?" ' "[1] The Self-affirmation "I am" comes before everything else, stands above and beyond all argument. No proof can make it stronger; no disproof can weaken it. Both proof and disproof found themselves on "I am," the unanalysable Feeling of mere Existence, of which nothing can be predicated except increase and diminution. "I am more" is the expression of Pleasure; "I am less" is the expression of Pain.

When we observe this "I am," we find that it expresses itself in three different ways: (*a*) The internal reflection of a Non-Self, KNOWLEDGE, the root of thoughts; (*b*) the internal concentration, WILL, the root of desires; (*c*) the going forth to the external, ENERGY, the root of actions; "I know" or "I think," "I will" or "I desire," "I energise" or "I act." These are the three affirmations

---

[1] *The Science of the Emotions*, p. 20.

of the indivisible Self, of the "I am." All manifestations may be classified under one or other of these three heads; the Self manifests in our worlds only in these three ways; as all colours arise from the three primaries, so the numberless manifestations of the Self all arise from Will, Energy, Knowledge.

The Self as Willer, the Self as Energiser, the Self as Knower—he is the One in Eternity and also the root of individuality in Time and Space. It is the Self in the Thought aspect, the Self as Knower, that we are to study.

THE NOT-SELF AS KNOWN

The Self whose "nature is knowledge" finds mirrored within himself a vast number of forms, and learns by experience that he cannot know and act and will in and through them. These forms, he discovers, are not amenable to his control as is the form of which he first becomes conscious, and which he (mistakenly, and yet necessarily) learns to identify with himself. He knows, and they do not think; he wills, and they show no desire; he energises, and there is no responsive movement in them. He cannot say *in them*, "I know," "I act," "I will"; and at length he recognises them as other selves, in mineral, vegetable, animal, human, and super-human forms, and he generalises all these under one comprehensive term, the Not-Self, that in which he, as a separated Self, is not, in which he does not know, and act, and will. He thus answers for a long time the question:

"What is the Not-Self?"

with

"All in which I do not know and will and act."

And although truly he will find, on successive
analyses, that his vehicles, one after another—save indeed, the finest film that makes him *a* Self—are
parts of the Not-Self, are objects of knowledge, are
the Known, not the Knower, for all practical purposes his answer is correct. In fact he can never
know, as divisible from himself, this finest film
that makes him a separated Self, since its presence
is necessary to that separation, and to know it as
the Not-Self would be to merge in the All.

KNOWING

In order that the Self may be the Knower and
the Not-Self the Known, a definite relationship must
be established between them. The Not-Self must
affect the Self, and the Self must in return affect
the Not-Self. There must be an interchange between
the two. Knowing is a relation between the Self
and the Not-Self, and the nature of that relation
must be the next division of our subject, but it is
well first to grasp clearly the fact that knowing is *a
relation*. It implies duality, the consciousness of a
Self and the recognition of a Not-Self—and the presence of the two set over against each other is necessary for knowledge.

The Knower, the Known, the Knowing—these are
the three in one which must be understood if thought-
power is to be turned to its proper purpose, the
helping of the world. According to Western ter-
minology, the Mind is the Subject which knows; the
Object is that which is known; the Relationship
between them is knowing. We must understand the
nature of the Knower, the nature of the Known, and
the nature of the relation established between them,

and how that relationship arises. These things understood, we shall indeed have made a step towards that Self-knowledge which is wisdom. Then, indeed, shall we be able to aid the world around us, becoming its helpers and saviours; for this is the true end of wisdom, that, set on fire by love, it may lift the world out of misery into the knowledge wherein all pain ceases for evermore. Such is the object of our study, for truly is it said in the books of that nation which possesses the earliest, and still the deepest and subtlest, psychology, that the object of philosophy is to put an end to pain. For that the Knower thinks; for that knowledge is continually sought. To put an end to pain is the final reason for philosophy, and that is not true wisdom which does not conduce to the finding of PEACE.

CHAPTER I

THE NATURE OF THOUGHT

THE nature of thought may be studied from two standpoints: from the side of consciousness, which is knowledge, or from the side of the form by which knowledge is obtained, the susceptibility of which to modifications makes possible the attainment of knowledge. This possibility has led to the two extremes in philosophy, both of which we must avoid, because each ignores one side of manifested life. One regards everything as consciousness, ignoring the essentiality of form as conditioning consciousness, as making it possible. The other regards everything as form, ignoring the fact that form can only exist by virtue of life ensouling it. The form and the life, the matter and the spirit, the vehicle and the consciousness, are inseparable in manifestation, and are the indivisible aspects of THAT in which both inhere, THAT which is neither consciousness nor its vehicle, but the ROOT of both. A philosophy which tries to explain everything by the forms, ignoring the life, will find problems it is utterly unable to solve. A philosophy which tries to explain everything by the life, ignoring the forms, will find itself faced by dead walls which it cannot surmount. The final word on this is that consciousness and its vehicles, life and form, spirit and matter, are the temporary expressions of the two aspects of the one unconditioned Existence, which is not known save when manifested as the Root-Spirit—(called by the Hindus Pratyagatman), the abstract Being, the abstract Logos—whence all individual selves, and the Root-Matter (Mulaprakriti) whence all forms. Whenever manifestation takes place this Root-Spirit gives birth to a triple consciousness, and this Root-Matter to a triple matter; beneath these is the One Reality, for ever incognisable by the conditioned consciousness. The flower sees not the root whence it grows, though all its life is drawn from it and without it it could not be.

The Self as Knower has as his characteristic function the mirroring within himself of the Not-Self. As a sensitive plate receives rays of light reflected from objects, and those rays cause modifications in the material on which they fall, so that images of the objects can be obtained, so is it with the Self in the aspect of knowledge towards everything external. His vehicle is a sphere whereon the Self receives from the Not-Self the reflected rays of the One Self, causing to appear on the surface of this sphere images which are the reflections of that which is not himself. The Knower does not know the things themselves in the earlier stages of his consciousness. He knows only the images produced in his vehicle by the action of the Not-Self on his responsive casing, the photographs of the external world. Hence the mind, the vehicle of the Self as Knower, has been compared to a mirror, in which are seen the images of all objects placed before it. We do not know the things themselves, but only the effect produced by them in our consciousness; not the objects, but the images of the objects, are what we find in the mind. As the mirror seems to have the objects within it, but those apparent objects are only images, illusions caused by the rays of light reflected from the objects, not the objects themselves; so does the mind, in its knowledge of the outer universe, know only the illusive images and not the things in themselves.

These images, made in the vehicle, are perceived as objects by the Knower, and this perception consists in his reproduction of them in himself. Now, the analogy of the mirror, and the use of the word "reflection" in the preceding paragraph, are a little misleading, for the mental image *is a reproduction not a reflection* of the object which causes it. The matter of the mind is actually shaped into a likeness of the object presented to it, and this likeness, in its turn, is reproduced by the Knower. When he thus modifies himself into the likeness of an external object, he is said *to know* that object, but in the case we are considering that which he knows is only the image produced by the object in his vehicle, and not the object itself. And this image is not a perfect reproduction of the object, for a reason we shall see in the next chapter.

"But," it may be said, "will that be so ever? Shall we never know the things in themselves?" This brings us to the vital distinction between the consciousness and the matter in which the consciousness is working, and by this we may find an answer to that natural question of the human mind. When the consciousness by long evolution has developed the power to reproduce within itself all that exists outside it, then the envelope of matter in which it has been working falls away, and the consciousness that is knowledge identifies its Self with all the Selves amid which it has been evolving, and sees at the Not-Self only the matter connected alike with all Selves severally. That is the "Day be with us," the union which is the triumph of evolution, when consciousness knows itself and others, and knows others as itself. By sameness of nature perfect knowledge is attained, and the Self realises that marvellous state where identity perishes not and mémory is not lost, but where separation finds its ending, and knower, knowing, and knowledge are one.

It is this wondrous nature of the Self, who is evolving in us through knowledge at the present time, that we have to study, in order to understand the nature of thought, and it is necessary to see clearly the illusory side in order that we may utilise the illusion to transcend it. So let us now study how Knowing—the relation between the Knower and the Known—is established, and this will lead us to see more clearly into the nature of thought.

THE CHAIN OF KNOWER, KNOWING, AND KNOWN

There is one word, vibration, which is becoming more and more the keynote of Western science, as it has long been that of the science of the East. Motion is the root of all. Life is motion; consciousness is motion. And that motion affecting matter is vibration. The One, the All, we think of as Changeless, either as Absolute Motion or as Motionless, since in One relative motion cannot be. Only when there is differentiation, or parts, can we think of what we call motion, which is change of place in succession of time. When the One becomes the Many, then motion arises; it is health, consciousness, life, when rhythmic, regular, as it is disease, unconsciousness, death, when without rhythm, irregular. For life and death are twin sisters, alike born of motion, which is manifestation.

Motion must needs appear when the One becomes the Many; since, when the omnipresent appears as separate particles, infinite motion must represent omnipresence, or, otherwise put, must be its reflection or image in matter. The essence of matter is separateness, as that of spirit is unity, and when the twain appear in the One, as cream in milk, the reflection of the omnipresence of that One in the multiplicity of Matter is ceaseless and infinite motion. Absolute motion—the presence of every moving unit at every point of space at every moment of time—is identical with rest, being only rest looked at in another way, from the standpoint of matter instead of from that of spirit. From the standpoint of spirit there is always One, from that of matter there are always Many.

This infinite motion appears as rhythmical movements, vibrations, in the matter which manifests it, each Jiva, or separated unit of consciousness, being isolated by an enclosing wall of matter from all other Jivas.[1] Each Jiva further becomes embodied, or clothed, in several garments of matter. As these garments of matter vibrate, they communicate their vibrations to the matter surrounding them, such matter becoming the medium wherein the vibra-

---

[1] There is no convenient English word for "a separated unit of consciousness"—"spirit" and "soul" connoting various peculiarities in different schools of thought. I shall therefore venture to use the name Jiva, instead of the clumsy "a separated unit of consciousness."

tions are carried outwards; and this medium, in turn, communicates the impulse of vibration to the enclosing garments of another Jiva, and thus sets that Jiva vibrating like the first. In this series of vibrations—beginning in one Jiva, made in the body that encircles it, sent on by the body to the medium around it, communicated by that to another body, and from that second body to the Jiva encircled by it—we have the chain of vibrations whereby one knows another. The second knows the first because he reproduces the first in himself, and thus experiences as he experiences. And yet with a difference. For our second Jiva is already in a vibratory condition, and his state of motion after receiving the impulse from the first is not a simple repetition of that impulse, but a combination of his own original motion with that imposed on him from without, and hence is not a perfect reproduction. Similarities are obtained, ever closer and closer, but identity ever eludes us, so long as the garments remain.

This sequence of vibratory actions is often seen in nature. A flame is a center of vibratory activity in ether, named by us heat; these vibrations, or heat-waves, throw the surrounding ether into waves like unto themselves, and these throw the ether in a piece of iron lying near into similar waves, and its particles vibrate under their impulse, and so the iron becomes hot and a source of heat in its turn. So does a series of vibrations pass from one Jiva to another, and all beings are interlinked by this network of consciousness.

So again in physical nature we mark off different ranges of vibrations by different names, calling one set light, another heat, another electricity, another sound, and so on; yet all are of the same nature, all are modes of motion in ether,[1] though they differ in rates of velocity and in the character of the waves. Thoughts, Desires, and Actions, the active manifestations in matter of Knowledge, Will, and Energy, are all of the same nature, that is, are all made up of vibrations, but differ in their phenomena, because of the different character of the vibrations. There is a series of vibrations in a particular kind of matter and with a certain character, and these we call thought-vibrations. Another series is spoken of as desire-vibrations, another series as action vibrations. These names are descriptive of certain facts in nature. There is a certain kind of ether thrown into vibration, and its vibrations affect our eyes; we call the motion light. There is another far subtler ether thrown into vibrations which are perceived, *i.e.*, are responded to, by the mind, and we call that motion thought. We are surrounded by matter of different densities and we name the motions in it as they affect ourselves, are answered to by different organs of our gross or subtle bodies. We name "light" certain motions affecting the eye; we name "thought" certain motions affecting another organ, the mind. "Seeing" occurs when the light-ether is thrown into waves from an object to our eye; "thinking" occurs when the thought-ether is thrown into waves between an object and our mind. The one is not more— nor less—mysterious than the other.

In dealing with the mind we shall see that modifications in the arrangement of its materials are caused by the impact of thought-waves, and that in concrete thinking we experience over again the

---

[1] Sound is also primarily an etheric vibration.

original impacts from without. The Knower finds his activity in these vibrations, and all to which they can answer, that is, all that they can reproduce, is Knowledge. The thought is a reproduction within the mind of the Knower of that which is not the Knower, is not the Self; it is a picture, caused by a combination of wave-motions, an image, quite literally. A part of the Not-Self vibrates and as the Knower vibrates in answer that part becomes the known; the matter quivering between them makes knowing possible by putting them into touch with each other. Thus is the chain of Knower, Known, and Knowing established and maintained.

CHAPTER II

THE CREATOR OF ILLUSION

"HAVING become indifferent to objects of perception, the pupil must seek out the Raja of the Senses, the Thought-Producer, he who awakes illusion.

"The Mind is the great slayer of the Real."

Thus is it written in one of the fragments translated by H. P. Blavatsky from *The Book of the Golden Precepts*, that exquisite prose-poem which is one of her choicest gifts to the world. And there is no more significant title of the mind than this: the "creator of illusion."

The mind is not the Knower, and should ever be carefully distinguished from him. Many of the confusions and the difficulties that perplex the student arise because he does not remember the distinction between him who knows and the mind which is his instrument for obtaining knowledge. It is as though the sculptor were identified with his chisel.

The mind is fundamentally dual and material, being made up of an envelope of fine matter, called the causal body and manas, the abstract mind, and of an envelope of coarser matter, called the mental body and manas, the concrete mind—manas itself being a reflection in atomic matter of that aspect of the Self which is Knowledge. This mind limits the Jiva, which, as self-consciousness increases, finds himself hampered by it on every side. As a man, to effect a certain purpose, might put on thick gloves, and find that his hands in them had lost much of their power of feeling, their delicacy of touch, their ability to pick up small objects, and were only capable of grasping large objects and of feeling heavy impacts, so is it with the Knower when he puts on the mind. The hand is there as well as the glove, but its capacities are greatly lessened; the Knower is there as well as the mind, but his powers are much limited in their expression.

We shall confine the term mind in the following paragraphs to the concrete mind—the mental body and manas.

The mind is the result of past thinking, and is constantly being modified by present thinking; it is a thing, precise and definite, with certain powers and incapacities, strength and weakness, which are the outcome of activities in previous lives. It is as we have made it; we cannot change it save slowly, we cannot transcend it by an effort of the will, we cannot cast it aside, nor instantaneously remove its imperfections. Such as it is, it is ours, a part of the Not-Self appropriated and shaped for our own using, and only through it can we know.

All the results of our past thinkings are present with us as mind, and each mind has its own rate of vibration, its own range of vibration, and is in a state of perpetual motion, offering an ever-changing series of pictures. Every impression coming to us from outside is made on this already active sphere, and the mass of existing vibrations modifies and is modified by the new arrival. The resultant is not, therefore, an accurate reproduction of the new vibration, but a combination of it with the vibrations already proceeding. To borrow again an illustration from light. If we hold a piece of red glass before our eyes and look at green objects, they will appear to us to be black. The vibrations that give us the sensation of red are cut off by those that give us the sensation of green, and the eye is deceived into seeing the object as black. So also if we look at a blue object through a yellow glass, shall we see it as black. In every case a coloured medium will cause an impression of colour different from that of the object looked at by the naked eye. Even looking at things with the naked eye, persons see them somewhat differently, for the eye itself modifies the vibrations it receives more than many people imagine. The influence of the mind as a medium by which the Knower views the external world is very similar to the influence of the coloured glass on the colours of objects seen through it. The Knower is as unconscious of this influence of the mind, as a man who had never seen, except through red or blue glasses, would be unconscious of the changes made by them in the colours of a landscape.

It is in the superficial and obvious sense that the mind is called the "creator of illusion." It presents us only with distorted images, a combination of itself and the external object. In a far deeper sense, indeed, is it the "creator of illusion," in that even these distorted images are but images of appearances, not of realities; shadows of shadows are all that it gives us. But it will suffice us at present to consider the illusions caused by its own nature.

Very different would be our ideas of the world, if we could know it as it is, even in its phenomenal aspect, instead of by means of the vibrations modified by the mind. And this is by no means impossible, although it can only be done by those who have made great progress in controlling the mind. The vibrations of the mind can be stilled, the consciousness being withdrawn from it; an impact from without will then shape an image exactly corresponding to itself, the vibrations being identical in quality and quantity, unintermixed with vibrations belonging to the observer. Or, the consciousness may go forth and ensoul the observed object, and thus directly experience its vibrations. In both cases a true knowledge of the form is gained. The idea in the world of noumena, of which the form expresses a phenomenal aspect, may also be known, but only by the consciousness working in the causal body, untrammelled by the concrete mind or the lower vehicles.

The truth that we only know our impressions of things, not the things—except as just stated—is one which is of vital moment when it is applied in practical life. It teaches humility and caution, and readiness to listen to new ideas. We lose our instinctive certainty that we are right in our observations, and learn to analyse ourselves before we condemn others.

An illustration may serve to make this more clear.

I meet a person whose vibratory activity expresses itself in a way complementary to my own. When we meet, we extinguish each other; hence we do not like each other, we do not see anything in each other, and we each wonder why So-and-so-thinks the other so clever, when we find each other so preternaturally stupid. Now, if I have gained a little self-knowledge, this wonder will be checked, so far as I am concerned. Instead of thinking that the other is stupid, I shall ask myself: "What is lacking in me that I cannot answer his vibrations? We are both vibrating, and if I cannot realise his life and thought, it is because I cannot reproduce his vibrations. Why should I judge him, since I cannot even know him until I modify myself sufficiently to be able to receive him?" We cannot greatly modify others, but we can greatly modify ourselves, and we should be continually trying to enlarge our receptive capacity. We must become as the white light in which all colours are present, which distorts none because it rejects none, and has in itself the power to answer to each. We may measure our approach to the whiteness by our power of response to the most diverse characters.

THE MENTAL BODY AND MANAS

We may now turn to the composition of the mind as an organ of consciousness in its aspect as Knower, and see what this composition is, how we have made the mind in the past, how we can change it in the present.

The mind on the side of life is manas, and manas is the reflection, in the atomic matter of the third —or mental—plane, of the cognitional aspect of the Self—of the Self as Knower.

On the side of form it presents two aspects, severally conditioning the activity of manas, the consciousness working on the mental plane. These aspects are due to the aggregations of the matter of the plane drawn round the atomic vibratory centre. This matter, from its nature and use, we term mind-stuff, or thought-stuff. It makes one great region of the universe, interpenetrating astral and physical matter, and exists in seven subdivisions, like the states of matter on the physical plane; it is predominantly responsive to those vibrations which come from the aspect of the Self which is Knowledge, and this aspect imposes on it its specific character.

The first—and higher—aspect of the form-side of mind is that called the causal body. It is composed of matter from the fifth and sixth subdivisions of the mental plane, corresponding to the finer ethers of the physical plane. The causal body is little developed in the majority at the present stage of evolution, as it remains unaffected by the mental activities directed to external objects, and we may, therefore, leave it aside, at any rate for the present. It is, in fact, the organ for abstract thought.

The second aspect is called the mental body, and is composed of thought-stuff belonging to the four lower subdivisions of the mental plane corresponding to the lowest ether, and the gaseous, liquid, and solid states of matter on the physical plane. It might indeed be termed the dense mental body. Mental bodies show seven great fundamental types, each of which includes forms at every stage of development, and all evolve and grow under the same laws. To understand and apply these laws is to change the slow evolution by nature to the rapid growth by the self-determining intelligence. Hence the profound importance of their study.

THE BUILDING AND EVOLUTION OF THE MENTAL BODY

The method by which consciousness builds up its vehicle is one which should be clearly grasped, for every day and hour of life gives opportunity for its application to high ends. Waking or sleeping, we are ever building our mental bodies; for when consciousness vibrates it affects the mind-stuff surrounding it, and every quiver of consciousness, though it be due only to a passing thought, draws into the mental body some particles of mind-stuff, and shakes out other particles from it. So far as the vehicle—the body—is concerned, this is due to the vibration; but it should not be forgotten that the very *essence* of consciousness is to constantly identify itself with the Not-Self, and as constantly to re-assert itself by rejecting the Not-Self; consciousness *consists* of the alternating assertion and negation, "I am this," "I am not this"; hence its motion is and causes, in matter, the attracting and repelling that we call a vibration. The surrounding matter is also thrown into waves, thus serving as a medium for affecting other consciousnesses.

Now, the fineness or coarseness of the matter thus appropriated depends on the quality of the vibrations set up by the consciousness. Pure and lofty thoughts are composed of rapid vibrations, and can only affect the rare and subtle grades of mind-stuff. The coarser grades remain unaffected, being unable to vibrate at the necessary speed. When such a thought causes the mental body to vibrate, particles of the coarser matter are shaken out of the body, and their place is taken by particles of the finer grades, and thus better materials are built into the mental body. Similarly, base and evil thoughts draw into the mental body the coarser materials suitable for their own expression, and these materials repel and drive out the finer kinds.

Thus these vibrations of consciousness are ever shaking out one kind of matter and building in another. And it follows, as a necessary consequence, that according to the kind of matter we have built into our mental bodies in the past, will be our power of responding to the thoughts which now reach us from outside. If our mental bodies are composed of fine materials, coarse and evil thoughts will meet with no response, and hence can inflict no injury; whereas if they are built up with gross materials, they will be affected by every evil passer-by, and will remain irresponsive to and unbenefited by the good.

When we come into touch with one whose thoughts are lofty, his thought-vibrations, playing on us, arouse vibrations of such matter in our mental bodies as is capable of responding, and these vibrations disturb and even shake out some of that which is too coarse to vibrate at his high rate of activity. The benefit we receive from him is thus largely dependent on our own past thinking, and our "understanding" of him, our responsiveness, is conditioned by these. We cannot think for each other; he can only think his own thoughts, thus causing corresponding vibrations in the mind-stuff around him, and these play upon us, setting up in our mental bodies sympathetic vibrations. These affect the consciousness. A thinker external to ourselves can only affect our consciousness by arousing these vibrations in our mental bodies.

But immediate understanding does not always follow on the production of such vibrations, caused from outside. Sometimes the effect resembles that of the sun and the rain and the earth on the seed that lies buried in the ground. There is no visible answer at first to the vibrations playing on the seed; but within there is a tiny quiver of the ensouling life, and that quiver will grow stronger and stronger day by day, till the evolving life bursts the seed-shell and sends forth rootlet and growing point. So with the mind. The consciousness thrills faintly within itself, ere it is able to give any external answer to the impacts upon it; and when we are not yet capable of understanding a noble thinker, there is yet in us an unconscious quivering which is the forerunner of the conscious answer. We go away from a great presence a little nearer to the rich thought-life flowing from it than we were ere we entered it, and germs of thought have been quickened in us, and our minds helped in their evolution.

Something, then, in the building and evolution of our minds may be done from outside, but most must result from the activities of our own consciousness; and if we would have mental bodies which should be strong, well-vitalised, active, able to grasp the loftier thoughts presented to us, then we must steadily work at right thinking; for we are our own builders, and fashion our minds for ourselves.

Many people are great readers. Now, reading does not build the mind; thought alone builds it. Reading is only valuable as it furnishes materials for thought. A man may read much, but his mental growth will be in proportion to the amount of thought that he expends in his reading. The value to him of the thought which he reads depends on the use he makes of it. Unless he takes up the thought and works on it himself, its value to him will be small and passing. "Reading makes a full man," said Lord Bacon, and it is with the mind as with the body. Eating fills the stomach, but as the meal is useless to the body unless it is digested and assimilated, so also the mind may be filled by reading, but unless there is thought; there is no assimilation of what is read, and the mind does not grow thereby—nay, it is likely to suffer from overloading, and to weaken rather than strengthen under a burden of unassimilated ideas.

We should read less, and think more, if we would have our minds grow, and our intelligence develop. If we are in earnest in the culture of our minds, we should daily spend an hour in the study of some serious and weighty book, and, reading for five minutes, we should think for ten, and so on through the hour. The usual way is to read quickly for the hour, and then to put away the book till the next hour comes for reading. Hence people grow very slowly in thought power.

The student eager for growth should resolve that no day shall pass that shall not have in it at least five minutes' reading and ten minutes' strenuous thinking on what is read. At first he will find the effort tiresome and laborious, and he will discover the weakness of his thinking power. This discovery marks his first step, for it is much to discover that one is unable to think hard and consecutively. People who cannot think, but who imagine that they can, do not make much progress. It is better to know one's weakness than to imagine oneself strong when one is feeble. The realisation of the weakness—the wandering of the mind, the feeling of heat, confusion, and fatigue which comes on in the brain after a prolonged effort to follow out a difficult line of thought, is on all fours with the similar feeling in the muscles after a strong muscular exertion. With regular and persistent—but not excessive—exercise, the thought-power will grow as the muscle-power grows. And as this thought-power grows, it also comes under control, and can be directed to definite ends. Without this thinking, the mental body will remain loosely formed and unorganised; and without gaining concentration—the power of fixing the thought on a definite point—thought-power cannot be exercised at all.

CHAPTER III

THOUGHT-TRANSFERENCE

ALMOST everyone nowadays is anxious to practise thought-transference, and dreams of the delights
of communicating with an absent friend without the
assistance of telegraph or post. Many people seem
to think that they can accomplish the task with
very little effort, and are quite surprised when they
meet with total failure in their attempts. Yet it is
clear that one must be able to think ere one can
transfer thought, and some power of steady thinking
must be necessary in order to send a thought-current
through space. The feeble vacillating thoughts of
the majority of people cause mere flickering vibrations in the thought-atmosphere, appearing and van-
ishing minute by minute, giving rise to no definite
form and endowed with the lowest vitality. A
thought-form must be clearly cut and well vitalised
if it is to be driven in any definite direction, and to
be strong enough, on arriving at its destination, to
set up there a reproduction of itself.

There are two methods of thought-transference,
one which may be distinguished as physical, the
other as psychical, one belonging to the brain as
well as the mind, the other to the mind only. A
thought may be generated by the consciousness, cause
vibration in the mental body, then in the astral body,
set up waves in etheric and then in the dense mole-

cules of the physical brain; by these brain vibrations
the physical ether is affected, and the waves pass outward, till they reach another brain and set up vibrations in its dense and etheric parts. By that receiving
brain vibrations are caused in the astral and then in
the mental bodies attached to it, and the vibrations
in the mental body draw out the answering quiver
in consciousness. Such are the many stages of the
arc traversed by a thought. But this traversing of a
"loopline" is not necessary. The consciousness may,
when causing vibrations in its mental body, direct
those vibrations straight to the mental body of the
receiving consciousness, thus avoiding the round just
described.

Let us see what happens in the first case.

There is a small organ in the brain, the pineal
gland, the function of which is unknown to Western
physiologists, and with which Western psychologists
do not concern themselves. It is a rudimentary organ in most people, but it is evolving, not retro-
grading, and it is possible to quicken its evolution
into a condition in which it can perform its proper
function, the function that, in the future, it will
discharge in all. It is the organ for thought-transference, as much as the eye is the organ of vision or the
ear of hearing.

If anyone thinks very intently on a single idea,
with concentration and sustained attention, he will
become conscious of a slight quiver or creeping
feeling—it has been compared to the creeping of an
ant—in the pineal gland. The quiver takes place in
the ether which permeates the gland, and causes a
slight magnetic current which gives rise to the creeping feeling in the dense molecules of the gland. If

the thought be strong enough to cause the current, then the thinker knows that he has been successful in bringing his thought to a pointedness and a strength which renders it capable of transmission.

That vibration in the ether of the pineal gland sets up waves in the surrounding ether, like waves of light, only much smaller and more rapid. These undulations pass out in all directions, setting the ether in motion, and these etheric waves, in turn, produce undulations in the ether of the pineal gland in another brain, and from that are transmitted to the astral and mental bodies in regular succession, thus reaching the consciousness. If this second pineal gland cannot reproduce these undulations, then the thought will pass unnoticed, making no impression, any more than waves of light make an impression on the eye of a blind person.

In the second method of thought-transference, the thinker, having created a thought-form on his own plane, does not send it down to the brain, but directs it immediately to another thinker on the mental plane. The power to do this deliberately implies a far higher mental evolution than does the physical method of thought-transference, for the sender must be self-conscious on the mental plane in order to exercise knowingly this activity.

But this power is being continually exercised by everyone of us indirectly and unconsciously, since all our thinkings cause vibrations in the mental body, that must, from the nature of things, be propagated through the surrounding mind-stuff. And there is no reason to confine the word thought-transference to conscious and deliberate transmissions of a particular thought from one person to another. We are all continually affecting each other by these waves of thought, sent out without definite intent, and what is called public opinion is largely created in this way. Most people think along certain lines, not because they have carefully thought a question out and come to a conclusion, but because large numbers of people are thinking along those lines, and carry others with them. The strong thought of a great thinker goes out into the world of thought, and is caught up by receptive and responsive minds. They reproduce his vibrations, and thus strengthen the thought-wave, affecting others who would have remained unresponsive to the original undulations. These, answering again, give added force to the waves, and they become still stronger, affecting large masses of people.

Public opinion, once formed, exercises a dominant sway over the minds of the great majority, beating unceasingly on all brains and awakening in them responsive undulations.

There are also certain national ways of thinking, definite and deeply cut channels, resulting from the continual reproduction during centuries of similar thoughts, arising from the history, the struggles, the customs of a nation. These profoundly modify and colour all minds born into the nation, and everything that comes from outside the nation is changed by the national vibration-rate. As thoughts that come to us from the outer world are modified by our mental bodies, and when we receive them we receive their vibrations *plus* our own normal vibrations—a resultant—so do nations, receiving impressions from other nations, receive them as modified by their own national vibration-rate. Hence people in different countries see the same facts, but add to them their own existing prepossessions, and quite honestly accuse each other of falsifying the facts and practising unfair methods. If this truth, and its inevitableness, were recognised, many international quarrels would be smoothed more easily than is now the case, many wars would be avoided, and those waged would be more easily put an end to. Then each nation would recognise what is sometimes called "the personal equation," and instead of blaming the other for difference of opinion, each would seek the mean between the two views, neither insisting wholly on its own.

The very practical question for the individual that arises from the knowledge of this continual and general thought-transference, is: How much can I gain of good, and avoid of evil, seeing that I must live in a mixed atmosphere, wherein good and evil thought-waves are ever active and are beating against my brain? How can I guard myself against injurious thought-transference, and how can I profit by the beneficial? The knowledge of the way in which the selective power works is of vital importance.

Each man is the person who most constantly affects his own mental body. Others affect it occasionally, but he always. The speaker to whom he listens, the author whose book he reads, affect his mental body. But they are incidents in his life; *he* is a permanent factor. His own influence over the composition of the mental body is far stronger than that of anyone else, and he himself fixes the normal vibration-rate of his mind. Thoughts which do not harmonise with that rate will be flung aside when they touch the mind. If a man thinks truth, a lie cannot make a lodgement in his mind; if he thinks love, hate cannot disturb him; if he thinks wisdom, ignorance cannot paralyse him. Here alone is safety, here real power. The mind must not be allowed to lie as it were fallow, for then any thought-seed may take root and grow; it must not be allowed to vibrate as it pleases, for that means that it will answer to any passing vibration.

There lies the practical lesson. The man who practises it will soon find its value, and will discover that by thinking, life can be made nobler and happier, and that it is true that by wisdom we can put an end to pain.

CHAPTER IV

THE BEGINNINGS OF THOUGHT

FEW outside the circle of students of psychology have troubled themselves much with the question: How does thought originate? When we now come into the world, we find ourselves possessed of a large amount of thought ready made, a large store of what are called "innate ideas." These are conceptions which we bring with us into the world, the condensed or summarised results of our experiences in lives previous to the present one. With this mental stock-in-hand we begin our transactions in this life, and the psychologist is never able to study by direct observation the beginnings of thought.

He can, however, learn something from the observation of an infant, for just as the new physical body runs over in pre-natal life the long physical evolution of the past, so does the new mental body swiftly traverse the stages of its long development. It is true that "mental body" is not by any means identical with "thought," and hence that even in studying the new mental body itself, we are not really studying the "beginnings of thought" at all; to a still greater degree is this true, when we consider that few people can study even the mental body directly, but are confined to the observation of the effects of the workings of that body on its denser fellow, the physical brain and nervous system. "Thought" is as distinct from the mental body as from the physical; it belongs to consciousness, to the life side, whereas mental and physical bodies belong *alike* to the form, to the matter side, and are mere transitory vehicles or instruments. As already said, the student must ever keep before him "the distinction between him who knows and the mind which is his instrument for obtaining knowledge," and the definition of the word "mind," already given, as "the mental body and manas"—a compound.

We can, however, by studying the effects of thought on these bodies, when the bodies are new, infer by correspondence something of the beginnings of thought, when a Self, in any given universe, comes first into contact with the Not-Self. The observations may help us, according to the axiom, "As above, so below." Everything here is but a reflection, and by studying the reflections, we may learn something of the objects that cause them.

If an infant be closely observed, it will be seen that sensations—response to stimuli by feelings of pleasure or pain, and primarily by those of pain—precede any sign of intelligence. That is, that vague sensations precede definite cognitions. Before birth, the infant was sustained by the life-forces flowing through the mother's body. On its being launched on an independent existence, these are cut off. Life flows away from the body and is not now renewed; as the life-forces lessen, want is felt, and this want is pain. The supply of the want gives ease, pleasure, and the infant sinks back into unconsciousness. Presently sights and sounds arouse sensation, but still no intellectual sign is given. The first sign of intelligence is when the sight or voice of the mother or nurse is connected with the satisfaction of the ever-recurring want, with the giving of pleasure by food; the linking together in, or by, memory of a group of recurring sensations with one external object, which object is regarded as separate from, and as the cause of, those sensations. Thought is the cognition of a relation between many sensations and a one, a unity, linking them together. This is the first expression of intelligence, the first thought—technically a "perception." The essence of this is the establishing of such a relation as is above described between a unit of consciousness—a Jiva—and an object, and wherever such a relation is established there thought is present.

This simple and ever-verifiable fact may serve as a general example of the beginning of thought in a separated Self—that is, in a triple Self encased in an envelope of matter, however fine, *a* Self as distinguished from *the* Self; in such a separated Self sensations precede thoughts; the attention of the Self is aroused by an impression made on him and responded to by a sensation. The massive feeling of want, due to the diminution of life-energy, does not by itself arouse thought; but that want is satisfied by the contact of the milk, causing a definite local impression, an impression followed by a feeling of pleasure. After this has been often repeated, the Self reaches outwards, vaguely, gropingly; outwards, because of the direction of the impression, which has come from outside. The life-energy thus flows into the mental body and vivifies it, so that it reflects—faintly at first—the object which, coming into contact with the body, has caused the sensation. This modification in the mental body, being repeated time after time, stimulates the Self in his aspect of knowledge, and he vibrates corresponden-tially. He has felt want, contact, pleasure, and with the contact an image presents itself, the eye being affected as well as the lips, two sense-impressions blending. His own inherent nature links these three, the want, the contact-image, the pleasure, together, and this link is thought. Not till he thus answers is there any thought; it is the Self that perceives, not any other or lower.

This perception specialises the lesire, which ceases to be a vague craving for something, and becomes a definite craving for a special thing—milk. But the perception needs revision, for the Knower has associated three things together, and one of them has to be disjoined—the want. It is significant that at an early stage the sight of the milk-giver arouses the want, the Knower calling up the want when the image associated with it appears; the child who is not hungry will cry for the breast on seeing the mother; later this mistaken link is broken, and the milk-giver is associated with the pleasure as cause, and seen as the object of pleasure. Desire for the mother is thus established, and then becomes a fur-ther stimulus to thought.

THE RELATION OF SENSATION AND THOUGHT

It is very clearly stated in many books on psychol-ogy, Eastern and Western, that all thought is rooted in sensation, that until a large number of sensations have been accumulated there can be no thinking. "Mind, as we know it," says H. P. Blavatsky, "is resolvable into states of consciousness, of varying du-ration, intensity, complexity, etc., all, in the ultimate,

resting on sensation."[1] Some writers have gone far-
ther than this, declaring that not only are sensations
the materials out of which thoughts are constructed,
but that thoughts are produced by sensations, thus
ignoring any Thinker, any Knower. Others, at the
opposite extreme, look on thought as the result of
the activity of the Thinker, initiated from within
instead of receiving its first impulse from without,
sensations being materials on which he employs his
own inherent specific capacity, but not a necessary
condition of his activity.

Each of the two views, that thought is the pure
product of sensations and that thought is the pure
product of the Knower, contains truth, but the full
truth lies between the two. While it is necessary
for the awakening of the Knower that sensations
should play upon him from without, and while the
first thought will be produced in consequence of
impulses from sensation, and sensations will serve as
its necessary antecedent; yet unless there were an
inherent capacity for linking things together, unless
the self were knowledge in his own nature, sensations might be presented to him continually and
never a thought would be produced. It is only half
the truth that thoughts have their beginning in sensations; there must work on the sensations the power
of organising them, and of establishing connecting
links, relations between them, and also between them
and the external world. The Thinker is the father,
Sensation the mother, Thought the child.

If thoughts have their beginnings in sensations,
and those sensations are caused by impacts from
without, then it is most important that when the

---

[1] *Secret Doctrine,* i, 31, *note.*

sensation arises, the nature and extent of that sensation shall be accurately observed. The first work of the knower is to observe; if there were nothing to observe he would always remain asleep; but when an object is presented to him, when as the Self he is conscious of an impact, then as Knower he observes. On the accuracy of that observation depends the thought which he is to shape out of many of these observations put together. If he observe inaccurately, if he establish a mistaken relation between the object that made the impact and himself who is observing the impact, then out of that error in his own work will grow a number of consequent errors that nothing can put right save going back to the very beginning.

Let us see now how sensation and perception work in a special case. Suppose I feel a touch on my hand, the touch causes, is answered by, a sensation; the recognition of the object which caused the sensation is a thought. When I feel a touch, I feel, and nothing more need be added as far as that pure sensation is concerned; but when from the feeling I pass to the object that caused the feeling, I perceive that object and the perception is a thought. This perception means that as Knower I recognise a relation between myself and that object, as having caused a certain sensation in my Self. This, however, is not all that happens. For I also experience other sensations, from colour, form, softness, warmth, texture; these are again passed on to me as Knower, and, aided by the memory of similar impressions formerly received, *i.e.*, comparing past images with the image of the object touching the hand—I decide on the kind of object that has touched it.

In this perception of things that make us feel, lies the beginning of thought; putting this into the ordinary metaphysical terms—the perception of a Not-Self as the cause of certain sensations in the Self is the beginning of cognition. Feeling alone, if such were possible, could not give consciousness of the Not-Self; there would be only the feeling of pleasure or pain in the Self, an inner consciousness of expansion or contraction. No higher evolution would be possible if a man could do nothing more than feel; only when he recognises objects as causes of pleasure or pain does his human education begin. In the establishing of a conscious relation between the Self and the Not-Self, the whole future evolution depends, and that evolution will largely consist in these relations becoming more and more numerous, more and more complicated, more and more accurate on the side of the Knower. The Knower begins his outer unfolding when the awakened consciousness, feeling pleasure or pain, turns its gaze on the external world and says: "That object gave me pleasure; that object gave me pain."

There must have been experienced a large number of sensations before the Self answers externally at all. Then comes a dull, confused groping after the pleasure, due to a desire in the willing Self to experience a repetition of the pleasure. And this is a good example of the fact mentioned before, that there is no such thing as pure feeling or pure thought; for "desire for the repetition of a pleasure" implies that the picture of the pleasure remains, however faintly, in the consciousness, and this is memory, and belongs to thought. For a long time the half-awakened Self drifts from one thing to another, striking against the Not-Self in haphazard fashion, without any direction being given to these movements by consciousness, experiencing pleasure and pain without any perception of the cause of either. Only when this has gone on for a long time is the perception above-mentioned possible, and the relation between the Knower and the Known begun.

CHAPTER V

MEMORY

THE NATURE OF MEMORY

WHEN a connection between a pleasure and a certain object is established, there arises the definite desire to again obtain that object, and so repeat the pleasure. Or, when a connection between a pain and a certain object is established, there arises a definite desire to avoid that object, and so escape the pain. On stimulation, the mental body readily repeats the image of the object; for, owing to the general law that energy flows in the direction of least resistance, the matter of the mental body is shaped most easily into the form already frequently taken; this tendency to repeat vibrations once started, when acted on by energy, is due to Tamas, to the inertia of matter, and is the germ of Memory. The molecules of matter, having been grouped together, fall slowly apart as other energies play on them, but retain for a considerable time the tendency to resume their mutual relation; if an impulse such as grouped them be given to them, they promptly fall again into position. Further, when the Knower has vibrated in any particular way, that *power of vibration* remains in him, and, in the case of the pleasure-giving, or pain-giving object, the desire for the object, or for avoiding the object, sets that power free, pushes it outwards, one might say, and thus gives the necessary stimulation to the mental body.

The image thus produced is recognised by the Knower, and in the one case the attachment caused by pleasure makes him reproduce also the image of the pleasure. In the other, the repulsion caused by pain equally causes the image of the pain. The object and the pleasure, or the object and the pain, are connected together in experience, and when the set of vibrations that compose the image of the object is made, the set of vibrations that make up the pleasure or the pain is also started, and the pleasure or the pain is retasted *in the absence of the object.* That is memory in its simplest form: a self-initiated vibration, of the same nature as that which caused the feeling of pleasure or pain, again causing that feeling. These images are less massive, and hence to the partially-developed Knower less vivid and living, than those caused by contact with an external object, heavy physical vibrations lending much energy to the mental and desire images, but fundamentally the vibrations are identical, and memory is the reproduction in mental matter by the Knower of objects previously contacted. This reflection may be—and is—repeated over and over again, in subtler and subtler matter, without regard to any separated Knower, and these in their totality are the partial contents of the memory of the Logos, the Lord of a Universe. These images of images may be reached by any separated Knower in proportion as he has developed within himself the "power of vibration" above mentioned. As in wireless telegraphy, a series of vibrations composing a message may be caught by any suitable receiver—*i.e.,* any receiver capable of reproducing them—so can a latent vibratory potency within a Knower be made active by a vibration similar to it in these cosmic images. These, on the akashic plane, form the "akashic records" often spoken of in Theosophical literature, and they last through the life of the system.

In order that we may clearly understand what lies at the root of "bad memory," we must examine the mental processes which go to make up what is called memory. Although in many psychological books memory is spoken of as a mental faculty, there is really no one faculty to which that name should be given. The persistence of a mental image is not due to any special faculty, but belongs to the general *quality* of the mind; a feeble mind is feeble in persistence as in all else, and—like a substance too fluid to retain the shape of the mould into which it has been poured—falls quickly out of the form it has taken. Where the mental body is little organised, is a mere loose aggregate of the molecules of mind-stuff, a cloud-like mass without much coherence, memory will certainly be very weak. But this weakness is general, not special; it is common to the whole mind, and is due to its low stage of evolution.

As the mental body becomes organised and the powers of the Jiva work in it, we yet often find what is called "a bad memory." But if we observe this "bad memory," we shall find that it is not faulty in all respects, that there are some things which are well remembered, and which the mind retains without effort. If we then examine these remembered things, we shall find that they are things which greatly attract the mind, that the things that are much liked are not forgotten. I have known a woman complain of a bad memory with respect to matters that were being studied, while I have observed in her a very retentive memory with regard to the details of a dress that she admired. Her mental body was not lacking in a fair amount of retentiveness, and when she observed carefully and attentively, producing a clear mental image, the image was fairly long-lived. Here we have the key to "bad memory." It is due to lack of attention, to lack of accurate observation, and therefore to confused thought. Confused thought is the blurred impression caused by careless observation and lack of attention, while clear thought is the sharply-cut impression due to concentrated attention and careful, accurate observation. We do not remember the things to which we pay little heed, but we remember well the things that keenly interest us.

How, then, should a "bad memory" be treated? First, the things should be noticed with regard to which it is bad and with regard to which it is good, so as to estimate the general quality of adhesiveness. Then the things with regard to which it is bad should be scrutinised, in order to see if they are worth remembering, and if they are things for which we do not care. If we find that we care little for them, but that in our best moments we feel we ought to care for them, then we should say to ourselves: "I will pay attention to them, will observe them accurately, and will think carefully and steadily on them." Doing this, we shall find our memory improve. For, as said above, memory is really dependent on attention, accurate observation, and clear thought; the element of attraction is valuable as fixing the attention, but if that be not present, its place must be taken by the will.

Now, it is just here that a very definite and widely-felt difficulty arises. How can "the will" take the place of the attraction? What is to move the will itself? Attraction arouses desire, and desire impels the moving towards the attractive object. This is, in the case supposed, absent. How is this absence of desire to be made good by the will? The will is the force prompting action when that force is determined in its direction by the deliberate Reason, and not by the influence of external objects felt as attractive. When the impulse to action, that which I have often called the outgoing energy of the Self, is motivated by external objects, is *drawn* forth, we call the impulse desire; when it is motivated by the Pure Reason, is *sent* forth, we call it will. What is needed then, in the absence of felt attraction from without, is illumination from within, and the motive for the will must be obtained by an intellectual survey of the field, and an exercise of the judgment as to the highest good, the goal of effort. That which the Reason selects as the thing most conducive to the good of the Self, serves as motive to the will. And when this has once been definitely done, then in moments of lassitude, of weakness, the recalling of the train of thought which led to the choice, again stimulates the will. Such a thing, deliberately chosen, may then be rendered attractive, *i.e.,* an object of desire, by setting the imagination to picture its pleasing qualities, the beneficial—happiness-giving—effects of its possession. But as he who wills an object wills the means, we become able to overcome the natural shrinking from effort and unpleasant discipline, by an exercise, thus motived, of the will. In the case under consideration, having determined that certain objects are eminently desirable as conducive to prolonged happiness, we set the will to work to carry out the activities which will lead to their obtaining.

In cultivating the power of observation, as in everything else, a little practice repeated daily is much more effective than a great effort followed by a period of inaction. We should set ourselves a little daily task of observing a thing carefully, imaging it in the mind *in all its details,* keeping the mind fixed on it for a short time, as the physical eye might be fixed on an object. On the following day we should call up the image, reproducing it as accurately as we can, and should then compare it with the object, and observe any inaccuracies. If we gave five minutes a day to this practice, alternately observing an object and picturing it in the mind, and recalling the previous day's image, and comparing our picture with the object, we should "improve our memory" very rapidly, and we should really be improving our powers of observation, of attention, of imagination, of concentration; in fact, we should be organising the mental body, and fitting it, far more rapidly than nature will fit it without assistance, to discharge its functions effectively and usefully. No man can take up such a practice as this, and remain unaffected by it; and he will soon have the satisfaction of knowing that his powers have increased, and that they have come much more under the control of the will.

The artificial ways of improving the memory present things to the mind in an attractive form, or associate with such a form the things to be remembered. If a person visualises easily, he will aid a bad memory by constructing a picture, and attaching to points in that picture the things he wants to remember; then the callng up of the picture brings up also the things that were to be remembered. Other people, in whom the auditory power is dominant, remember by the jingle of rhymes, and, for instance, weave a series of dates, or other unattractive facts, into verses that "stick in the mind." But far better than any of these ways is the rational method detailed above, by the use of which the mind-body becomes better organised, more coherent as to its materials.

MEMORY AND ANTICIPATION

Let us return to our undeveloped Knower.

When memory begins to function anticipation quickly follows, for anticipation is only memory thrown forwards. When memory gives the retasting of a pleasure experienced in the past, desire seeks to again grasp the object which gave the pleasure, and when this retasting is thought of as the result of finding that object in the outer world and enjoying it, we have anticipation. The image of the object and the image of the pleasure are dwelt on by the Knower in relation to each other; if he adds to this contemplation the element of time, of past and future, two names are given to such contemplation: the contemplation *plus* the idea of the past is memory, *plus* the idea of the future it is anticipation.

As we study these images, we begin to understand the full force of the aphorism of Patanjali, that for the practice of Yoga a man must stop the "modifications of the thinking principle." Looked at from the standpoint of occult science, every contact with the Not-Self modifies the mental body. Part cf the stuff of which that body is composed is re-arranged as a picture or image of the external object. When relations are established between these images, that is thinking, as seen on the form side. Correspondent with this are vibrations in the Knower himself, and these modifications within himself are thinking as seen on the life-side. It must not be forgotten that the establishing of these relations is the peculiar work of the Knower, his addition to the images, and that this addition changes the images into thoughts. The pictures in the mental body very much resemble in their character the impressions made on a sensitive plate by the etheric waves which lie beyond the light spectrum and which act chemically on the silver salts, re-arranging the matter on the sensitive plate, so that pictures are formed on it of the objects to which it has been exposed. So on the sensitive plate that we call the mental body, the materials are re-arranged as a picture of the objects that have been contacted. The Knower perceives these pictures by his own responsive vibrations, studies them, and after a while begins to arrange them and to modify them by the vibrations he sends out on them from himself. By the law already spoken of, that energy follows the line of least resistance; he re-forms over and over again the same images, makes images of images; so long as he confines himself to this simple reproduction, with the sole addition of the time-element, we have, as said, memory and anticipation.

Concrete thinking is, after all, only a repetition in subtler matter of every-day experiences, with this difference, that the Knower can stop and change their sequence, repeat them, hurry or slacken them as he will. He can delay on any image, brood over it, dwell on it, and can thus gain from his leisurely re-examination of experiences much that had escaped him as he passed through them, bound to the un-resting, unhasting wheel of time. Within his own domain, he can make his own time, so far as its measures are concerned, as does the Logos for His worlds; only he cannot escape from the essence of time, succession, until he can touch the Logic con-sciousness, freeing himself from the bonds of the world-matter; and then, even, only so far as this system is concerned.

CHAPTER VI

THE GROWTH OF THOUGHT

OBSERVATION AND ITS VALUE

THE first requisite for competent thinking is attentive and accurate observation. The Self as Knower must observe the Not-Self with attention and with accuracy, if it is to become the Known, and thus merge in the Self.

The second requisite is receptivity and tenacity in the mental body, the power of yielding quickly to impressions and of retaining them when made.

In proportion to the attention and accuracy of the Knower's observation, and the receptivity and tenacity of his mental body, will be the rapidity of his evolution, the speed at which his latent potencies become active powers.

If the Knower has not accurately observed the thought-image, or if the mental body, being undeveloped, has been insensitive to all but the stronger vibrations of an external object, and so has been modified into an imperfect reproduction, the material for thought is inadequate and misleading. The broad outline is at first all that is obtained, the details being blurred or even omitted. As we evolve our faculties, and as we build finer stuff into the mental body, we find that we receive from the same

external object much more than we received in our
undeveloped days. Thus we find much more in an
object than we found in it before.

Let two men stand in a field, in presence of a
splendid sunset. Let one of these be an agricultural
labourer, who has not been in the habit of observing
nature save with reference to his crops, who has
only looked at the sky to see if it promises rain or
sunshine, caring nothing for its aspects save as they
bear on his own livelihood and employment. Let
the second be an artist, a painter of genius, full of
the love of beauty, and trained to see and enjoy every
shade and tone of colour. The labourer's physical,
astral, and mental bodies are all in presence of that
gorgeous sunset, and all the vibrations caused by it
are playing upon the vehicles of his consciousness; he
sees different colours in the sky, and observes that
there is much red, promising a fine day for the
morrow, good or bad for his crops, as the case may
be. This is all he gets out of it. The painter's
physical, astral, and mental bodies are all exposed
to exactly the same pulsations as those of the labourer,
but how different is the result! The fine material
of his bodies reproduces a million vibrations too
rapid and subtle to move the coarse material of the
other. His image of the sunset is consequently quite
different from the image produced in the labourer.
The delicate shades of colour, hue melting into hue,
translucent blue and rose and palest green lighted
with golden gleams and flecked with royal purple—
all these are tasted with a lingering joy, an ecstasy
of sensuous delight; there are waked all fine emotions, love and admiration merging into reverence
and joy that such beauty can be; ideas of the most

inspiring character arise, as the mental body modifies itself under the vibrations playing on it on the mental plane from the mental aspects of the sunset. The difference of the images is not due to an external cause, but to an internal receptivity. It does not lie in the outside, but in the capacity to respond. It is not in the Not-Self, but in the Self and its sheaths. According to these differences is the result produced; how little flows into the one, how much into the other!

Here we see with startling force the meaning of the evolution of the Knower. A universe of beauty may be around us, its waves playing on us from every side, and yet for us it may be non-existent. Everything that is in the mind of the Logos of our system is playing on us and on our bodies now. How much of it we can receive marks the stage of our evolution. What is wanted for growth is not a change without us, but a change within us. Everything is already given us, but we have to develop the capacity to receive.

It will be gathered from what has just been said that one element in clear thinking is accurate observation. We have to begin this work on the physical plane, where our bodies come into contact with the Not-Self. We climb *upwards,* and all evolution begins on the lower plane and passes on into the higher; on the lower we first touch the external world, and thence the vibrations pass upwards—or inwards—calling out the inner powers.

Accurate observation, then, is a faculty to be definitely cultivated. Most people go through the world with their eyes half closed, and we can each test this for ourselves by questioning ourselves on what we have observed while passing along a street. We can ask: "What have I observed while walking down this street?" Many persons will have observed next to nothing, no clear images have been formed. Others will have observed a few things; some will have observed many. It is related by Houdini that he trained his child in observing the contents of the shops he passed, walking along the streets of London, until he could give the whole contents of a shop-front which he had passed by without stopping, having thrown over it a mere glance. The normal child is observant, and according to the extent of his capacity for observation is the measure of his intelligence. The habit of clear, quick observation lies in the average man at the root of clear thinking. Those who think most confusedly are generally those who observe least accurately: except where intelligence is highly developed and is turned inwards habitually, and the bodies have not been trained in the way spoken of below.

But the answer to the above question may be: "I was thinking of something else, and therefore did not observe." And the answer is a good one, if the answerer was thinking of something more important than the training of the mental body and of the power of attention by careful observation. Such a one may have done well in his lack of observation; but if the answerer has only been dreaming, drifting about aimlessly, then he has wasted his time much more than if he had turned his energy outwards.

A man deeply engaged in thought will be unobservant of passing objects, turned inwards and not outwards, and will not attend to what is going on before him. It may not be worth his while, in this life, to train his bodies to make quasi-independent observations, for the highly developed and the partially developed need different training.

But how many of the unobservant people are really "deeply engaged in thought?" In most people's minds all that is going on is an idle looking at any thought-image that happens to present itself, a turning over of the contents of the mind in an aimless fashion, as an idle woman turns over the contents of her wardrobes or her jewel-box. This is not thinking, for thinking means, as we have seen, the establishing of relations, the adding of something not previously present. In thinking, the attention of the Knower is deliberately directed to the thought-images, and he exerts himself actively upon them.

The development, then, of the habit of observation is part of the training of the mind, and those who practise it will find that the mind becomes clearer, increases in power, and becomes more easily manageable, so that they can direct it on any given object much better than they had been able previously to do. Now, this power of observation, once definitely established, works automatically, the mental and other bodies registering images which are available if wanted later, without calling at the time on the attention of their owner. It is, then, no longer necessary that the attention of the person should be directed to objects presented to the sense-organs in order that an impression of those objects may be made and preserved. A very trivial but significant case of this kind happened in my own experience. While I was travelling in America, a question arose one day about the number on the engine of a train by which we had been travelling. The number was instantly presented to me by my mind, but this was not, in any sense, a case of clairvoyance. For clairvoyant perception it would have been necessary to have hunted up the train and looked for the number. Without any conscious action on my part, the sense-organs, senses, and mind had observed and registered the number as the train came into the station, and when the number was wanted the mental image of the incoming train, with the number on the front of the engine, at once came up. This faculty, once established, is a useful one, for it means that when things that have been passing around you have not attracted your attention at the time, you can none the less recall them by looking at the record which the mental, astral, and physical bodies have made of them on their own account.

This automatic activity of the mental body, outside the conscious activity of the Jiva, goes on, however more extensively in all of us than might be supposed; for it has been found that when a person is hypnotised he will report a number of small events which had passed him by without arousing his attention. These impressions reach the mental body through the brain, and are impressed on the latter as well as on the former. Many impressions thus reach the mental body that are not sufficiently deep to enter into consciousness—not because consciousness cannot cognise them, but because it is not normally awake enough to notice any but the deeper impressions. In the hypnotic trance, in delirium, in physical dreams, when the Jiva is away, the brain yields up these impressions, which are usually overpowered by the far stronger impressions received by and made by the Jiva himself; but if the mind is trained to observe and record, then the Jiva can recover from it, at will, the impressions thus made.

Thus, if two people walked down a street, one trained in observation and the other not, both would receive a number of impressions, and neither might be conscious of the receipt of these at the time; but afterwards, the trained observer would be able to recover these impressions, while the other would not. As this power lies at the root of clear thinking, those who desire to culture and control thought-power will do well to cultivate the habit of observation, and to sacrifice the mere pleasure of drifting idly along whithersoever the stream of fancy may carry them.

THE EVOLUTION OF MENTAL FACULTIES

As images accumulate, the work of the Knower becomes more complicated, and his activity upon them draws out one power after another, inherent in his divine nature. He no longer accepts the external world only in its simple relation to himself, as containing objects that are causes of pleasure or pain to himself; but he arranges side by side the images representing them, studies them in their various aspects, shifts them about, and reconsiders them. He begins also to arrange his own observations. He observes, when one image brings up another, the order of their succession. When a second has followed a first many times, he begins to look for the second when the first appears, and thus links the two together. This is his first attempt at reasoning, and here again we have the calling out of an inherent faculty. He argues that because A and B have always appeared successively, *therefore* when A appears B will appear. This forecast being continually verified, he comes to link them together as "cause" and "effect," and many of his early errors are due to a too hasty establishment of this relation. Further, setting images side by side, he observes their unlikenesses and likenesses, and develops a power of comparison. He chooses one or another as pleasure-giving, and moves the body in search of them in the external world, developing judgment by these selections and their consequences. He evolves a sense of proportion in relation to the likenesses and unlikenesses, and groups objects together by their prominent likenesses, separating them from others by their prominent unlikenesses; here also he makes many errors, corrected by later observations, being easily misled at first by surface similarities.

Thus observation, discrimination, reason, comparison, judgment, are evolved one after another, and these faculties grow with exercise, and thus the aspect of the Self as Knower is developed by the activity of thoughts, by the action and re-action continually repeated between the Self and the Not-Self.

To quicken the evolution of these faculties, we must deliberately and consciously exercise them, using the circumstances of daily life as opportunities for developing them. Just as we saw that the power of observation might be trained in everyday life, so can we accustom ourselves to see the points of likeness and unlikeness in the objects round us, we can draw conclusions and test them by events, we can compare, and judge, and all this consciously and of set purpose. Thought-power grows rapidly under this deliberate exercise, and becomes a thing that is consciously wielded, felt as a definite possession.

THE TRAINING OF THE MIND

To train the mind in any one direction is to train it altogether to some extent, for any definite kind of training organises the mind-stuff of which the mental body is composed, and also calls out some of the powers of the Knower. The increased capacity can be directed to any end, and is available for all purposes. A trained mind can be applied to a new subject, and will grapple with it and master it in a way impossible to the untrained, and this is the use of education.

But it should always be remembered that the training of the mind does not consist in cramming it with facts, but in drawing out its powers. The mind does not grow by being gorged with other people's thoughts, but by exercising its own faculties. It is said of the great Teachers who stand at the head of human evolution that They know everything which exists within the solar system. This does not mean that every fact therein is always within Their consciousness, but that they have so developed the aspect of knowledge in Themselves that whenever They turn Their attention in any direction, They know the object to which it is turned. This is a much greater thing than the storage in the mind of any number of facts, as it is a greater thing to see any object on which the eye is turned than to be blind and to know it only by the description given of it by others. The evolution of the mind is measured not by the images it contains, but by the development of the nature which is knowledge, the power to reproduce within itself anything that is presented to it. This will be as useful in any other universe as in this, and once gained is ours to use wherever we may be.

Now, this work of training the mind may be very much helped forward by coming into touch with those who are more highly evolved than ourselves. A thinker who is stronger than we are can materially aid us, for he sends out vibrations of a higher order than we are able to create. A piece of iron lying on the ground cannot start heat-vibrations on its own account; but if it happens to be placed near a fire, it can answer to the heat-vibrations of the fire, and thus become hot. When we come near a strong thinker, his vibrations play on our mental bodies and set up in them corresponding vibrations, so that we vibrate sympathetically with him. For the time being we feel that our mental power is increased and that we are able to grasp conceptions that normally elude us. But when we are again alone, we find that these very conceptions have become blurred and confused.

People will listen to a lecture, and follow it intelligently, for the time being understanding the teaching it conveys. They go away satisfied, feeling that they have made a substantial gain in knowledge. On the following day, wishing to share with a friend what had been gained, they find to their mortification that they cannot reproduce the conceptions which seemed to be so clear and luminous. Often they will exclaim impatiently: "I am sure I know it; it is there, if I could only get hold of it." This feeling arises from the memory of the vibrations which both mental body and Jiva have experienced; there is the consciousness of having realised the conceptions, the memory of the forms taken, and the feeling that, having produced them, reproduction should be easy. But on the previous day it was the masterful vibrations of the stronger thinker that shaped the forms taken by the mental body; they were moulded from without, not from within. The sense of inability experienced on the attempt to reproduce them means that this shaping must be done for them a few times, before they will have sufficient strength to reproduce those forms by self-initiated vibrations. The Knower must have vibrated in these higher ways several times, ere he can reproduce the vibrations at will. By virtue of his own inherent nature he can evolve the power within himself to reproduce them, when he has been made to answer several times by impact from without. The power in both Knowers is the same, but one has evolved it, while in the other it is latent. It is brought out of latency by the contact with a similar power already in activity, and thus the stronger quickens the evolution of the weaker.

Herein lies one of the values of associating with persons more advanced than ourselves. We profit by their contact, and grow under their stimulating influence. A true Teacher will thus aid his disciples far more by keeping them near him than by any spoken words.

For this influence direct personal contact affords the most effective channel. But failing this, or in association with it, much may also be gained from books, if the books be wisely chosen. In reading the work of a really great writer, we should try for the time to put ourselves into a negative or receptive condition, so as to receive as many of his thought-vibrations as possible. When we have read the words, we should dwell on them, ponder over them, try to sense the thought they partially express, draw out of them all their hidden relationships. Our attention must be concentrated, so as to pierce the mind of the writer through the veil of his words. Such reading serves as an education, and helps forward our mental evolution. Less strenuous reading may serve as a pleasant pastime, may store our minds with valuable facts, and so subserve our usefulness. But such reading as is described means a stimulus to our evolution, and should not be neglected by those who seek to grow in order to serve.

CHAPTER VII

CONCENTRATION

FEW things more tax the powers of the student who is beginning to train his mind than does concentration. In the early stages of the activity of the mind, progress depends on its swift movements, on its alertness, on its readiness to receive impacts from sensation after sensation, turning its attention quickly from one to another. Versatility is, at that stage, a most valuable quality, and the constant turning outwards of the attention is essential to progress. While the mind is collecting materials for thought, extreme mobility is an advantage, and for many, many lives the mind grows through this mobility, and increases it by exercise. The stoppage of this habit of running outwards in every direction, the imposition of fixed attention on a single point—this change naturally comes with a jar and a shock, and the mind plunges wildly, like an unbroken horse when it first feels the bit.

We have seen that the mental body is shaped into images of the objects towards which attention is directed. Patanjali speaks of stopping the modifications of the thinking principle, *i.e.,* of stopping these ever-changing reproductions of the outer world. To stop the ever-changing modifications of the mental body, and to keep it shaped to one steady image, is concentration so far as the form is concerned; to direct the attention steadily to this form so as to reproduce it perfectly within itself is concentration so far as the Knower is concerned.

In concentration, the consciousness is held to a single image; the whole attention of the Knower is fixed on a single point, without wavering or swerving. The mind—which runs continually from one thing to another, attracted by external objects and shaping itself to each in swift succession—is checked, held in, and forced by the will to remain in one form, shaped to one image, disregarding all the impressions thrown upon it.

Now, when the mind is thus kept shaped to one image, and the Knower steadily contemplates it, he obtains a far fuller knowledge of the object than he could obtain by means of any verbal description of it. Our idea of a picture, or a landscape, is far more complete when we have seen it, than when we have only read of it, or heard it described. And if we concentrate on such a description the picture is shaped in the mental body, and we gain a fuller knowledge of it than is gained by mere reading of the words. Words are symbols of things, and concentration on the rough outline of a thing produced by a word descriptive of it fills in more and more detail, as the consciousness comes more closely into touch with the thing described.

It must be remembered that concentration is not a state of passivity, but, on the contrary, one of intense and regulated activity. It resembles, in the mental world, the gathering up of the muscles for a spring in the physical world, or their stiffening to meet a prolonged strain. In fact, this tension always shows itself in a corresponding physical tension with beginners, and physical fatigue follows the exercise of concentration—fatigue of the muscles, not only of nervous system. As fixing the eye steadily on an object enables us to observe its details, unnoticed in a hasty glance, so does concentration enable us to observe the details of an idea. And as we increase the intensity of the concentration, we take in more in the time, as a runner passes more objects in a minute than does a walker. The walker will expend exactly the same amount of muscular energy in passing twenty objects as will the runner, but the swifter pouring out of energy corresponds to the shorter time of passage.

At the beginning of concentration two difficulties have to be overcome. First, this disregard of the impressions continually being thrown on the mind. The mental body must be prevented from answering these contacts, and the tendency to respond to these outside impressions must be resisted; but this necessitates the partial direction of the attention to the resistance itself, and when the tendency to respond has been overcome the resistance itself must pass: perfect balance is needed, neither resistance nor non-resistance, but a steady quietude so strong that waves from outside will not produce any result, not even the secondary result of the consciousness of something to be resisted.

Secondly, the mind itself must hold as sole image, for the time, the object of concentration; it must not only refuse to modify itself in response to impacts from without, but must also cease its own inner activity, wherewith it is constantly re-arranging its contents, thinking over them, establishing new relations, discovering hidden likenesses and unlikenesses.

It has now to confine its attention to a single object, to fix itself on that. It does not, of course, cease its activity, but sends it all along a single channel. Water flowing over a surface wide in comparison with the amount of water will have little motor power. The same water sent along a narrow channel, with the same initial impulse, will carry away an obstacle. Hence the value of the "one-pointedness" so continually insisted on by the teachers of meditation. Without adding to the strength of the mind, the *effective* strength of it is immensely increased. Steam allowed to expand in the free air does not move a midge out of its path; but along a pipe, the same steam would drive a piston. This imposition of inner stillness is even more difficult than the ignoring of outside impacts, being concerned with its own deeper and fuller life. To turn the back on the outside world is more easy than to quiet the inner, for this inner world is more identified with the Self, and, in fact, to most people at the present stage of evolution, represents the "I." The very attempt, however, thus to still the mind soon brings about a step forward in the evolution of consciousness, for we quickly feel that the Ruler and the ruled cannot be one. and instinctively identify ourselves with the Ruler. "*I* quiet *my* mind," is the expression of the consciousness, and the mind is felt as belonging to, as a possession of, the "I."

This distinction grows up unconsciously, and the student finds himself becoming conscious of a duality, of something which is controlling, and something which is controlled. The lower concrete mind is separated off, and the "I" is felt as of greater power, clearer vision, and there is evolved a feeling that this

"I" is not dependent on either body or mind. This is the first realisation, *i.e., feeling,* in consciousness of the true immortal nature, already intellectually seen as existing, such vision having, in fact, prompted the very concentration which is thus rewarded As the practice goes on, the horizon widens out, but as though inwards, not outwards, inwards and inwards continually, illimitably. There unfolds a power of knowing Truth at sight, which only shows itself when the mind, with its slow processes of reasoning, is transcended. [The reader must never forget that "the mind" is used throughout as meaning "the lower mind," the mental body, *plus* manas.] For the "I" is the expression of the Self whose nature is knowledge, and whenever he comes into contact with a truth, he finds its vibrations regular, and therefore capable of producing a coherent image in himself, whereas the false causes a distorted image, out of proportion, by its very reflection announcing its nature. As the mind assumes a more and more subordinate position, these powers of the Ego assert their own predominance, and intuition—analogous to the direct vision of the physical plane—takes the place of reasoning, which may perhaps be compared to the physical plane sense of touch. In fact, the analogy is closer than at the first glance may appear. For intuition develops out of reasoning in the same unbroken manner, and without change of essential nature, as the eye develops out of touch. There is certainly a great change of "manner," but this should not blind us to the orderly and sequential evolution. The intuition of the unintelligent is impulse, born of desire, and is lower, not higher, than reasoning.

When the mind is well trained in concentrating

on an object, and can maintain its one-pointedness
—as this state is called—for some little time, the next
stage is to drop the object, and to maintain the mind
in this attitude of fixed attention *without the atten-
ion being directed to anything*. In this state the
mental body shows no image; its own material is
there, held steady and firm, receiving no impressions,
in a condition of perfect calm, like a waveless lake.
This is not a state which can last for more than
a *very* brief period, like the "critical state" of the
chemist, the point of contact between two recognised
and defined sub-states of matter. Otherwise put, the
consciousness, as the mental body is stilled, escapes
from it, and passes into and out of the "laya centre,"
the neutral points of contact between the mental
body and the causal body; the passage is accompanied
by a momentary swoon, or loss of consciousness—the
inevitable result of the disappearance of objects of
consciousness—followed by consciousness in the higher. The dropping out of objects of consciousness belonging to the lower worlds is thus followed by the
appearance of objects of consciousness in the higher.
Then can the Ego shape that mental body according
to his own lofty thoughts and permeate it with his
own vibrations. He can mould it after the high
visions of the planes beyond his own, that he has
caught a glimpse of in his own highest moments, and
can thus convey downwards and outwards ideas to
which the mental body would otherwise be unable
to respond. These are the inspirations of genius,
that flash down into the mind with dazzling light,
and illuminate a world. The very man who gives
them to the world can scarce tell in his ordinary
mental state how they have reached him; only he

knows that in some strange way

> ". . . . . . the power within me pealing
> Lives on my lip and beckons with my hand."

CONSCIOUSNESS IS WHEREVER THERE IS AN OBJECT TO WHICH IT RESPONDS

In the world of form, a form occupies a definite place, and cannot be said to be—if the expression may be pardoned—in a place where it is not. That is, occupying a certain place, it is closer to or more distant from other forms also occupying certain places in relation to its own. If it would change from one place to another, it must cross over the intervening space; the transit may be swift or slow, rapid as the lightning flash, sluggish as the tortoise, but it must be made, and it occupies some time, whether the time be brief or long.

Now, with regard to consciousness, space has no such existence. Consciousness changes its state, not its place, and embraces more or less, knows or does not know of that which is not itself, just in proportion as it can or cannot answer to the vibrations of the not-selves. Its horizon enlarges with its receptivity, *i.e.*, with its power of response, with its power to reproduce vibrations. In this there is no question of travelling, of crossing over intermediate intervals. Space belongs to forms, which affect each other most when near each other, and whose power over each other diminishes as their distance from each other increases.

All successful students in concentration re-discover for themselves this non-existence of space for consciousness. An Adept can acquire knowledge of any object within His limit by concentrating upon it, and distance in no way affects such concentration. He becomes conscious of an object, say on another planet, not because his astral vision acts telescopically, but because in the inner region the whole universe exists as a point; such a man reaches the Heart of Life, and sees all things therein.

It is written in the Upanishads that within the heart there is a small chamber, and therein is the "inner ether," which is co-extensive with space; this is the Atma, the Self, immortal, beyond grief:

"Within this abide the sky and the world; within this abide fire and air, the sun and the moon, the lightning and the stars, all that is and all that is not in This [the universe]."[1]

This "inner ether of the heart" is an ancient mystic term descriptive of the subtle nature of the Self, which is truly one and all-pervading, so that anyone who is conscious in the Self is conscious at all points of the universe. Science says that the movement of a body here affects the farthest star, because all bodies are plunged in, interpenetrated by, ether, a continuous medium which transmits vibrations without friction, therefore without loss of energy, therefore to any distance. This is on the form side of Nature. How natural, then, that consciousness, the life side of Nature, should be similarly all-pervading and continuous.

We feel ourselves to be "here" because we are receiving impressions from the objects around us. So when consciousness vibrates in response to "distant" objects as fully as to "near" objects, we feel ourselves to be with them. If consciousness responds to an event taking place in Mars as fully as to an

---

[1] *Chhandogyopanishat* VIII. i. 3.

event taking place in our own room, there is no difference in its knowledge of each, and it feels itself as "here" in each case equally. There is no question of place, but a question of evolution of capacity. The Knower is wherever his consciousness can answer, and increase in his power to respond means inclusion within his consciousness of all to which he responds, of all that is within his range of vibration.

Here again physical analogy is helpful. The eye sees all which can send into it light-vibrations, and nothing else. It can answer only within a certain range of vibrations; all beyond that range, above or below it, is to it darkness. The old Hermetic axiom: "As above so below," is a clue in the labyrinth which surrounds us, and by a study of the reflection below we can often learn something of the object above which causes that reflection.

One difference between this power of being conscious at any place and "going to" the higher planes is that in the first case the Jiva, whether encased in its lower vehicles or not, feels himself at once in presence of the "distant" objects, and in the second, clothed in the mental and astral bodies, or in the mental only, travels swiftly from point to point and is conscious of translation. A far more important difference is that in the second case the Jiva may find himself in the midst of a crowd of objects which he does not in the least understand, a new and strange world which bewilders and confuses him; while in the first case he understands all he sees, and knows in every case the life as well as the form. Thus studied, the light of the One Self shines through all, and a serene knowledge is enjoyed which

---

[1] *Bhagavad Gita,* ii. 66.

can never be gained by spending numberless ages amid the wilderness of forms.

Concentration is the means whereby the Jiva escapes from the bondage of forms and enters the Peace. "For him without concentration there is no peace," quoth the Teacher,[1] for peace hath her nest on a rock that towers above the tossing waves of form.

HOW TO CONCENTRATE

Having understood the theory of concentration, the student should begin its practice.

If he be of a devotional temperament, his work will be much simplified, for then he can take the object of his devotion as the object of contemplation, and the heart being powerfully attracted to that object, the mind will readily dwell on it, presenting the beloved image without effort and excluding others with equal ease. For the mind is continually impelled by desire, and serves constantly as the minister of pleasure. That which gives pleasure is ever being sought by the mind, and it ever seeks to present images that give pleasure and to exclude those that give pain. Hence it will dwell on a beloved image, being steadied in that contemplation by the pleasure experienced in it, and if forcibly dragged away from it will return to it again and again. A devotee can then very readily reach a considerable degree of concentration; he will think of the object of his devotion, creating by the imagination, as clearly as he can, a picture, an image of that object, and he will then keep his mind fixed on that image, on the thought of the Beloved. Thus a Christian would think of the Christ, of the Virgin-Mother, of his Patron Saint, of his Guardian Angel; a Hindu would think of Maheshvara, of Vishnu, of Uma, of Shri Krishna; a Buddhist would think of the Buddha, of the Bodhisattva; a Parsi of Ahuramazda, of Mithra; and so on. Each and all of these objects appeal to the devotion of the worshipper, and the attraction exercised by them over the heart binds the mind to the happiness-giving object. In this way the mind becomes concentrated with the least exertion, the least loss of effort.

Where the temperament is not devotional, the element of attraction can still be utilized as a help, but in this case it will bind to an Idea not to a Person. The earliest attempts at concentration should always be made with this help. With the non-devotional the attractive image will take the form of some profound idea, some high problem; such should form the object of concentration, and on that the mind should be steadily bent. Herein the binding power of attraction is intellectual interest, the deep desire for knowledge, one of the profoundest loves of man.

Another very fruitful form of concentration, for one who is not attracted to a personality as an object of devotion, is to choose a virtue and concentrate upon that. A very real kind of devotion may be aroused by such an object, for it appeals to the heart through the love of intellectual and moral beauty. The virtue should be imaged by the mind in the completest possible way, and when a general view of its effects has been obtained, the mind should be steadied on its essential nature. A great subsidiary advantage of this kind of concentration is that as the mind shapes itself to the virtue and repeats its vibrations, the virtue will gradually be-

come part of the nature, and will be firmly established in the character. This shaping of the mind
is really an act of self-creation, for the mind after a
while falls readily into the forms to which it has
been constrained by concentration, and these forms
become the organs of its habitual expression. True
is it, as written of old:

Man is the creation of thought; what he thinks upon
in this life, that, hereafter, he becomes.[1]

When the mind loses hold of its object, whether
devotional or intellectual—as it will do, time after
time—it must be brought back, and again directed
to the object. Often at first it will wander away
without the wandering being noticed, and the student suddenly awakes to the fact that he is thinking
about something quite other than the proper object
of thought. This will happen again and again, and
he must patiently bring it back—a wearisome and
tiring process, but there is no other way by which
concentration can be gained.

It is a useful and instructive mental exercise, when
the mind has thus slipped away without notice, to
take it back again by the road along which it
travelled in its strayings. This process increases the
control of the rider over his runaway horse, and
thus diminishes its inclination to escape.

Consecutive thinking, though a step towards concentration, is not identical with it, for in consecutive
thinking the mind passes from one to another of a
sequence of images, and is not fixed on one alone.
But as it is far easier than concentration, the beginner may use it to lead up to the more difficult task.

---

[1] *Chhandogyopanishat*, III, xiv, i.

It is often helpful for a devotee to select a scene from the life of the object of his devotion, and to picture the scene vividly in its details, with local surroundings of landscape and colour. Thus the mind is gradually steadied on one line, and it can be led to and finally fixed on the central figure of the scene, the object of devotion. As the scene is reproduced in the mind, it takes on a feeling of reality, and it is quite possible in this way to get into magnetic touch with the record of that scene on a higher plane— the permanent photograph of it in the cosmic ether —and thus to obtain very much more knowledge of it than is supplied by any description of it that may have been given. Thus also may the devotee come into magnetic touch with the object of devotion and enter by this direct touch into far more intimate relations with him than are otherwise possible. For consciousness is not under the physical space-limitations, but *is* wheresoever it is conscious—a statement that has already been explained.

Concentration itself, however, it must be remembered, is not this sequential thinking, and the mind must finally be fastened to the one object and remain fixed thereunto, not reasoning on it, but, as it were, sucking out, absorbing, its content.

CHAPTER VIII

OBSTACLES TO CONCENTRATION

WANDERING MINDS

THE universal complaint which comes from those who are beginning to practise concentration is that the very attempt to concentrate results in a greater restlessness of the mind. To some extent this is true, for the law of action and reaction works here as everywhere, and the pressure put on the mind causes a corresponding reaction. But while admitting this, we find, on closer study, that the *increased* restlessness is largely illusory. The feeling of such increased restlessness is chiefly due to the opposition suddenly set up between the Ego, willing steadiness, and the mind in it normal condition of mobility. The Ego has, for a long series of lives, been carried about by the mind in all its swift movements, as a man is ever being carried through space by the whirling earth. He is not conscious of movement; he does not know that the world is moving, so thoroughly is he part of it, moving as it moves. If he were able to separate himself from the earth and stop his own movement without being shivered into pieces, he would only then be conscious that the earth was moving at a high rate of speed. So long as a man is yielding to every movement of the mind, he does not realise its continual activity and restlessness; but when he steadies himself, when he ceases to move, then he feels the ceaseless motion of the mind he has hitherto obeyed.

If the beginner knows these facts, he will not be discouraged at the very commencement of his efforts by meeting with this universal experience, but will, taking it for granted, go quietly on with his task. And, after all, he is but repeating the experience voiced by Arjuna five thousand years ago:

This Yoga which Thou hast declared to be by equanimity, O slayer of Madhu, I see no stable foundation for it, owing to restlessness; for the mind is verily restless, O Krishna! it is impetuous, strong, and difficult to bend; I deem it as hard to curb as the wind.

And still is true the answer, the answer pointing out the *only* way to success:

Without doubt, O mighty-armed, the mind is hard to curb and restless; but it may be curbed by constant practice and by indifference.[1]

The mind thus steadied will not be so easily thrown off its balance by the wandering thoughts from other minds, ever seeking to effect a lodgment, the vagrant crowd which continually encircles us. The mind used to concentration retains always a certain positiveness, and is not readily shaped by unlicensed intruders.

All people who are training their minds should maintain an attitude of steady watchfulness with regard to the thoughts that "come into the mind," and should exercise towards them a constant selection. The refusal to harbour evil thoughts, their prompt ejection if they effect an entry, the immediate replacement of an evil thought by a good one of the opposite character—this practice will so tune the mind that after a time it will act automatically,

---

[1] *Bhagavad-Gita,* vi 35,36.

repelling the evil of its own accord. Harmonious, rhythmical vibrations repel the inharmonious and irregular; they fly off from the rhythmically vibrating surface as a stone that strikes against a whirling wheel. Living, as we all do, in a continual current of thoughts, good and evil, we need to cultivate the selective action of the mind, so that the good may be automatically drawn in, the evil automatically repelled.

The mind is like a magnet, attracting and repelling, and the nature of its attractions and repulsions can be determined by ourselves. If we watch the thoughts which come into our minds, we shall find that they are of the same kind as those which we habitually encourage. The mind attracts the thoughts which are congruous with its normal activities. If we, then, for a time, deliberately practise selection, the mind will soon do this selection for itself on the lines laid down for it, and so evil thoughts will not penetrate into the mind, while the good will ever find an open door.

Most people are only too receptive, but the receptivity is due to feebleness, not to deliberate self-surrender to the higher influences. It is, therefore, well to learn how we may render ourselves normally positive, and how we may become negative when we decide that it is desirable that we should be so.

The habit of concentration will by itself tend to strengthen the mind, so that it will readily exercise control and selection with regard to the thoughts that come to it from outside, and it has already been stated how it can be trained automatically to repel the bad. But it may be well to add to what has been said, that when an evil thought enters the mind, it is better not to fight with it directly, but to utilize the fact that the mind can think of only one thing at a time; let the mind be at once turned to a good thought, and the evil one will be necessarily expelled. In fighting against anything, the very force we send out causes a corresponding reaction, and thus increases our trouble; whereas the turning of the mental eye to an image in a different direction causes the other image to drop silently from the field of vision. Many a man wastes years in combating impure thoughts, when quiet occupation of the mind with pure ones would leave no room for his assailants; further, as the mind thus draws to itself matter which does not respond to the evil, he is gradually becoming positive, unreceptive, to that kind of thought.

This is the secret of right receptivity; the mind responds according to its constitution; it answers to all that is of like nature with itself; we make it positive towards evil, negative towards good, by habitual good thinking, thus building into its very fabric materials that are receptive of good, unreceptive of evil. We must think of that which we desire to receive, and refuse to think of that which we desire not to receive. Such a mind, in the thought-ocean which surrounds it, draws to itself the good thoughts, repels the evil, and thus ever grows purer and stronger amid the very same thought conditions which render another fouler and weaker.

The method of replacing one thought by another is one that may be utilised to great advantage in many ways. If an unkind thought about another person enter the mind, it should at once be replaced by a thought of some virtue he possesses, of some good action he has done. If the mind is harassed by anxiety, turn it to the thought of the purpose that runs through life, the Good Law which "mightily and sweetly ordereth all things." If a particular kind of undesirable thought persistently obtrude itself then it is wise to provide a special weapon; some verse or phrase that embodies the opposite idea should be chosen, and whenever the objectionable thought presents itself, this phrase should be repeated and dwelt upon. In a week or two the thought will cease to trouble.

It is a good plan constantly to furnish the mind with some high thought, some word of cheer, some inspiration to noble living. Ere we go forth into life's turmoil day by day, we should give the mind this shield of good thought. A few words are enough, taken from some Scripture of the race, and this, fixed in the mind by a few recitations in the early morning, will recur to the mind again and again during the day, and will be found repeating itself in the mind, whenever the mind is disengaged.

THE DANGERS OF CONCENTRATION

There are certain dangers connected with the practice of concentration as to which the beginner should be warned, for many eager students, in their wish to go far, go too fast, and so hinder themselves instead of helping.

The body is apt to suffer owing to the ignorance and inattention of the student.

When a man concentrates his mind, his body puts itself into a state of tension, and this is not noticed by him, is involuntary so far as he is concerned. This following of the mind by the body may be noticed in very many trivial things; an effort to remember causes a wrinkling of the forehead, the eyes are fixed, and the eyebrows drawn down; tense attention is accompanied by fixity of the eyes, anxiety by an eager, wistful gaze. For ages, effort of the mind has been followed by effort of the body, the mind being directed entirely towards the supply of bodily needs by bodily exertions, and thus an association has been set up, which works automatically.

When concentration is commenced, the body, according to its wont, follows the mind, and the muscles become rigid and the nerves tense; hence great physical fatigue, muscular and nervous exhaustion, acute headache, are very apt to follow in the wake of concentration, and thus people are led to give it up, believing that these ill effects are inevitable.

As a matter of fact they can be avoided by a simple precaution. The beginner should now and again break off his concentration sufficiently to notice the state of his body, and if he finds it strained, tense, or rigid, he should at once relax it; when this has been done several times, the links of association will be broken, and the body will remain pliant and resting while the mind is concentrated. Patanjali said that in meditation the posture adopted should be "easy and pleasant"; the body cannot help the mind by its tension, and it injures itself.

Perhaps a personal anecdote may be pardoned as an illustration. One day, while under H. P. Blavatsky's training, I was desired by her to make an effort of the will; I did do so with much intensity, and with the result of much swelling in the blood-vessels of of the head. "My dear," she said drily, "you do not will with your blood-vessels."

Another physical danger arises from the effect

produced by concentration on the nerve-cells of the brain. As the power of concentration increases, as the mind is stilled, and the Ego begins to work through the mind, he makes a new demand on the brain nerve-cells. These cells are, of course, ultimately constituted of atoms, and the walls of these atoms consist of whorls of spirillae, through which run currents of life-energy. Of these spirillae there are seven sets, four only of which are in use; the remaining three are as yet unused—practically rudimentary organs. As the higher energies pour down, seeking a channel in the atoms, the set of spirillae which—later in evolution—will serve as their channel is forced into activity. If this be done very slowly and carefully, no harm results, but over-pressure means injury to the delicate structure of the spirillae. These minute, delicate tubes, when unused, have their sides in contact, like tubes of soft india-rubber; if the sides are violently forced apart, rupture is apt to result. The feeling of dullness and heaviness all over the brain is the danger-signal; if this be disregarded acute pain will follow, and obstinate inflammation may ensue. Concentration should therefore be practised very sparingly at first, and should never be carried to the point of brain-fatigue. A few minutes at a time is enough for a beginning, the time being lengthened gradually as the practice goes on.

But, however short the time which is given to it, it should be given regularly; if a day's practice be missed the previous condition of the atom reasserts itself, and the work has to be re-commenced. Steady and regular, but not prolonged, practice ensures the best results and avoids danger. In some schools of what is called Hatha Yoga the students are recommended to assist concentration by fixing the eyes on a black spot on a white wall, and to maintain this fixity of gaze until trance supervenes. Now, there are two reasons why this should not be done. First, the practice, after a while, injures the physical sight, and the eyes lose their power of adjustment. Secondly, it brings about a form of brain paralysis. This begins with the fatigue of the retinal cells, as the waves of light beat on them, and the spot disappears from view, the place on the retina where its image is formed becoming insensitive, the result of prolonged response. This fatigue spreads inwards, until finally a kind of paralysis supervenes, and the person passes into a hypnotic trance. In fact, excessive stimulation of a sense-organ is, in the West, a recognised means for producing hypnosis—the revolving mirror, the electric light, etc., being used with this object.

But brain paralysis not only stops all thinking on the physical plane, but renders the brain insensitive to non-physical vibrations, so that the Ego cannot impress it; it does not set him free, but merely deprives him of his instrument. A man may remain for weeks in a trance thus induced, but when he awakes he is no wiser than at the beginning of the trance. He has not gained knowledge; he has merely wasted time. Such methods do not gain spiritual power, but merely bring about physical disability.

MEDITATION

Meditation may be said to have been already explained, for it is only the sustained attitude of the concentrated mind in face of an object of devotion, of a problem that needs illumination to be intelligible, of anything whereof the life is to be realized and absorbed, rather than the form.

Meditation cannot be effectively performed until concentration is, at least partially, mastered. For concentration is not an end, but a means to an end; it fashions the mind into an instrument which can be used at the will of the owner. When a concentrated mind is steadily directed to any object, with the view of piercing the veil, and reaching the life, and drawing that life into union with the life to which the mind belongs—then meditation is performed. Concentration might be regarded as the shaping of the organ, meditation as its exercise. The mind has been made one-pointed; it is then directed to and dwells steadily on any object of which knowledge is desired.

Anyone who determines to lead a spiritual life must daily devote some time to meditation. As soon may the physical life be sustained without food as the spiritual without meditation. Those who cannot spare half an hour a day during which the world may be shut out and the mind may receive from the spiritual planes a current of life, cannot lead the spiritual life.

Only to the mind concentrated, steady, shut out from the world, can the Divine reveal itself. God shows Himself in His universe in endless forms; but within the human heart He shows Himself in His Life and Nature, revealing Himself to that which is a fragment to Himself. In that silence, peace and strength and force flow into the soul, and the man of meditation is ever the most efficient man of the world.

Lord Rosebery, speaking of Cromwell, described him as "a practical mystic," and declared that a practical mystic is the greatest force in the world. It is true. The concentrated intelligence, the power of withdrawing outside the turmoil, mean immensely increased energy in work, mean steadiness, self-control, serenity; the man of meditation is the man who wastes no time, scatters no energy, misses no opportunity. Such a man governs events, because within him is the power whereof events are only the outer expression; he shares the divine life, and therefore shares the divine power.

CHAPTER IX

THE STRENGTHENING OF THOUGHT POWER

WE may now proceed to turn our study of Thought Power to practical account, for study that does not lead to practice is barren. The old declaration still holds good: "The end of philosophy is to put an end to pain." We are to learn to develop and then to use our developed thought power to help those around us, the living and the so-called dead, to quicken human evolution, and to hasten also our own progress.

Thought power can only be increased by steady and persistent exercise; as literally and as truly as muscular development depends on the exercise of the muscles we already possess, so does mental development depend on the exercise of the mind already ours.

It is a law of life that growth results from exercise. The life, our Self, is ever seeking increased expression outwardly by means of the form in which it is contained. As it is called out by exercise, its pressure on the form causes the form to expand, and fresh matter is laid down in the form, and part of the expansion is thus rendered permanent. When the muscle is stretched by exercise more life flows into it, the cells multiply, and the muscle thus grows. When the mental body vibrates under the action of thought, fresh matter is drawn in from the mental atmosphere, and is built into the body, which thus increases in size as well as in complexity of structure. A mental body continually exercised grows, whether the thought carried on in it be good or evil. The amount of the thought determines the growth of the body, the quality of the thought determines the kind of matter employed in that growth.

Both the mental body and the physical brain grow by exercise, and those who would improve and enlarge them must have recourse to regular daily thinking, with the deliberately chosen object of improving their mental capacities. Needless to add that the inherent powers of the Knower are also evolved more rapidly by this exercise, and ever play upon the vehicles with increasing force.

In order that it may have its full effect this practice should be methodical. Let a man choose an able book on some subject which is attractive to him, a book written by a competent author, containing, fresh strong thought. A sentence, or a few sentences, should be read slowly, and then the reader should think closely and intently over what he has read. It is a good rule to think twice as long as one reads, for the object of the reading is not simply to acquire new ideas, but to strengthen the thinking faculties. Half an hour should be given to this practice if possible, but the student may begin with a quarter of an hour, as he will find the close attention a little exhausting at first.

Any person who takes up this practice and follows it regularly for a few months will at the end of that time be conscious of a distinct growth of mental strength, and he will find himself able to deal with the ordinary problems of life far more effectively than heretofore. Nature is a just paymistress, giving to each exactly the wages he has earned, but not an unearned farthing. Those who would have the wages of increased faculty must earn them by hard thinking.

The work is twofold, as has been already pointed out. On the one side the powers of consciousness are drawn out; on the other the forms through which it is expressed are developed; and the first of these must never be forgotten. Many people recognize the value of definite thinking as affecting the brain, but forget that the source of all thought is the unborn, undying Self, and that they are only drawing out what they already possess. Within them is all power, and they have only to utilize it, for the divine Self is the root of the life of each, and the aspect of the Self which is knowledge lives in everyone, and is ever seeking opportunity for his own fuller expression. The power is within each, uncreate, eternal; the form is moulded and changed, but the life is the man's Self, illimitable in his powers. That power within each is the same power as shaped the universe; it is divine, not human, a portion of the life of the Logos, and inseparate from Him.

If this were realized, and if the student remembered that it is not the scantiness of the power but the inadequacy of the instrument that makes the difficulty, he would often work with more courage and hope, and therefore with more efficiency. Let him feel that his essential nature is knowledge, and that it lies with him how far that essential nature shall find expression in this incarnation. Expression is, indeed, limited by the thinkings of the past, but can be now increased and made more efficient by the same power which in that past shaped the present. Forms are plastic and can be re-moulded, slowly, it is true, by the vibrations of the life.

Above all, let the student remember that for steady growth, regularity of practice is essential. When a day's practice is omitted, three or four days' work are necessary to counter-balance the slipping back, at least during the earlier stages of growth. When the *habit* of steady thought is acquired, then the regularity of practice is less important. But until this habit is definitely established, regularity is of the utmost moment, for the old habit of loose drifting re-asserts itself, and the matter of the mental body falls back into its old shapes, and has to be again shaken out of them on the resumption of the practice. Better five minutes of work done regularly, than half an hour on some days and none on others.

WORRY—IT'S MEANING AND ERADICATION

It has been said truly enough that people age more by worry than by work. Work, unless excessive, does not injure the thought-apparatus, but, on the contrary, strengthens it. But the mental process known as "worry" definitely injures it, and after a time produces a nervous exhaustion and irritability which render steady mental work impossible.

What is "worry"? It is the process of repeating the same train of thought over and over again with small alterations, coming to no result, and not even aiming at the reaching of a result. It is the continued reproduction of thought-forms, initiated by the mental body and the brain, not by the consciousness, and imposed by them on the consciousness. As overtired muscles cannot keep still, but move restlessly even against the will, so do the tired mental body and brain repeat over and over again the very vibrations that have wearied them, and the Thinker vainly tries to still them and thus obtain rest. Once more automatism is seen, the tendency to move in the direction in which movement has already been made. The Thinker has dwelt on a painful subject, and has endeavoured to reach a definite and useful conclusion. He has failed and ceases to think, but remains unsatisfied, wishing to find a solution, and dominated by the fear of the anticipated trouble. This fear keeps him in an anxious and restless condition, causing an irregular outflow of energy. Then the mental body and brain, under the impulse of this energy and of the wish, but undirected by the Thinker, continue to move and throw up the images already shaped and rejected. These are, as it were, forced on his attention, and the sequence recurs again and again. As weariness increases irritability is set up, and reacts again on the wearied forms, and so action and reaction continue in a vicious circle. The Thinker is, in worry, the slave of his servant-bodies, and is suffering under their tyranny.

Now, this very automatism of the mental body and brain, this tendency to repeat vibrations already produced, may be used to correct the useless repetition of thoughts that cause pain. When a thought-current has made for itself a channel—a thought-form —new thought currents tend to flow along the same track, that being the line of least resistance. A thought that causes pain readily thus recurs by the fascination of fear, as a thought that gives pleasure recurs by the fascination of love. The object of fear, the picture of what will happen when anticipation becomes reality, makes thus a mind-channel, a mould for thought, and a brain-track also. The tendency of the mental body and the brain, released from immediate work, is to repeat the form, and to let unemployed energy flow into the channel already made.

Perhaps the best way to get rid of a "worry-channel" is to dig another, of an exactly opposite character. Such a channel is, as we have already seen, made by definite, persistent, regular thought. Let, then, a person, who is suffering from worry, give three or four minutes in the morning, on first rising, to some noble and encouraging thought: "The Self is Peace; that Self am I. The Self is Strength; that Self am I." Let him think how, in his innermost nature, he is one with the Supreme Father; how in that nature he is undying, unchanging, fearless, free, serene, strong; how he is clothed in perishable vestures that feel the sting of pain, the gnawing of anxiety; how he mistakenly regards these as himself. As he thus broods, the Peace will enfold him, and he will feel it is his own, his natural atmosphere.

As he does this, day by day, the thought will dig its own channel in mental body and in brain, and ere long, when the mind is loosed from labour, the thought of the Self that is Peace and Strength will present itself unbidden, and fold its wings around the mind in the very turmoil of the world. Mental energy will flow naturally into this channel, and worry will be of the past.

Another way is to train the mind to rest on the Good Law, thus establishing a habit of content. Here the man dwells on the thought that all circumstances work within the Law, and that naught happens by chance. Only that which the Law brings to us can reach us, by whatever hand it may outwardly come. Nothing can injure us that is not our due, brought to us by our own previous willing and acting; none can wrong us, save as an instrument of the Law, collecting a debt due from us. Even if an anticipation of pain or trouble come to the mind, we will do well to face it calmly, accept it, agree to it. Most of the sting disappears when we acquiesce in the finding of the Law, whatever it may be. And we may do this the more easily if we remember that the Law works ever to free us, by exacting the debts that keep us in prison, and though it bring us pain, the pain is but the way to happiness. All pain, come it how it may, works for our ultimate bliss, and is but breaking the bonds which keep us tried to the whirling wheel of births and deaths.

When these thoughts have become habitual, the mind ceases to worry, for the claws of worry can find no hold on that strong panoply of peace.

THINKING AND CEASING TO THINK

Much gain of strength may be made by learning both to think and to cease thinking at will. While we are thinking we should throw our whole mind into the thought, and think our best. But when the work of thought is over, it should be dropped *completely*, and not allowed to drift on vaguely touching the mind and leaving it, like a boat knocking itself against a rock. A man does not keep a machine running when it is not turning out work, needlessly wearing the machinery. But the priceless machinery of the mind is allowed to turn and turn aimlessly, wearing itself out without useful result. To learn to cease thinking, to let the mind rest, is an acquisition of the greatest value. As the tired limbs luxuriate when stretched in repose, so may the tired mind find comfort in complete rest. Constant thinking means constant vibration; constant vibration means constant waste. Exhaustion and premature decay result from this useless expenditure of energy, and a man may preserve both mental body and brain longer by learning to cease thinking, when thought is not being directed to useful result.

It is true that "ceasing to think" is by no means an easy achievement. Perhaps it is even more difficult than thinking. It must be practised for very brief periods until the habit is established, for it means at first an expenditure of force in holding the mind still. Let the student, when he has been thinking steadily, drop the thought, and as any thought appears in the mind turn the attention away from it. Persistently turn away from each intruder; if need be, imagine a void, as a step to quiescence, and try to be conscious only of stillness and darkness. Practice on these lines will become more and more intelligible if persisted in, and a sense of quiet and peace will encourage the student to persist.

Nor should it be forgotten that the cessation of thought, busied in outward activities, is a necessary preliminary to work on the higher planes. When the brain has learned to be quiescent, when it no longer restlessly throws up the broken images of past activities, then the possibility opens of the withdrawal of the consciousness from its physical vesture, and of its free activity in its own world. Those who hope to take this forward step within the present life must learn to cease thinking, for only when "the modifications of the thinking principle" are checked on the lower plane can freedom on the higher be obtained.

Another way of giving the rest to the mental body and the brain—a far easier way than the cessation of thinking—is by change of thought. A man who thinks strenuously and persistently along one line should have a second line of thought, as different as possible from the first, to which he can turn his mind for refreshment. The extraordinary freshness and youthfulness of thought which characterized William Ewart Gladstone in his old age was largely the result of the subsidiary intellectual activities of his life. His strongest and most persistent thought went to politics, but his studies in theology and in Greek filled many a leisure hour. Truly he was but an indifferent theologian, and what he was as a Greek scholar I am not competent to say; but though the world cannot be said to be much the richer for his theological pronouncements, his own brain was kept fresh and receptive by these and his Grecian studies. Charles Darwin, on the other hand, lamented in his old age that he had allowed those of his faculties to atrophy by disuse, that would have been concerned with subjects outside his own specialized work. Literature and art for him had no attraction, and he keenly felt the limitations he had imposed on himself by his over-absorption in one line of study. A man needs change of exercise in thought as well as in body, else he may suffer from mental cramp as do some from writer's cramp.

Especially, perhaps, is it important for men engaged in absorbing worldly pursuits, that they should take up a subject which engages faculties of the mind not evolved in business activities, related to art, science, or literature, in which they may find mental recreation and polish. Above all, the young should adopt some such pursuit, ere yet their fresh and active brains grow jaded and weary, and in age they will then find within themselves resources which will enrich and brighten their declining days. The form will preserve its elasticity for a much longer period of time when it is thus given rest by change of occupation.

THE SECRET OF PEACE OF MIND

Much of that which we have already studied tells us something of the way in which peace of mind may be ensured. But its fundamental necessity is the clear recognition and realization of our place in the universe.

We are part of one great Life, which knows no failure, no loss of effort or strength, which "mightily and sweetly ordering all things" bears the worlds onwards to their goal. The notion that our little life is a separate independent unit, fighting for its own hand against countless separate independent units, is a delusion of the most tormenting kind. So long as we thus see the world and life, peace broods far off on an inaccessible pinnacle. When we feel and know that all selves are one, then peace of mind is ours without any fear of loss.

All our troubles arise from thinking of ourselves as separated units, and then revolving on our own mental axes, thinking only of our separate interests, our separate aims, our separate joys and sorrows. Some do this as regards the lower things of life, and they are the most dissatisfied of all, ever restlessly snatching at the general stock of material goods, and piling up useless treasures. Others seek ever their own separate progress in the higher life, good earnest people, but ever discontented and anxious. They are ever contemplating and analysing themselves: "Am I getting on? Do I know more than I did last year?" and so on, fretting for continual assurances of progress, their thoughts centred on their own inner gain.

Peace is not to be found in the continual seeking for the gratification of the separated self, even though the gratification be of the higher kind. It is found in renouncing the separated self, in resting on the Self that is One, the Self that is manifesting at *every* stage of evolution, and in our stage as much as in every other, and is content in all.

Desire for spiritual progress is of great value so long as the lower desires entangle and fetter the aspirant; he gains strength to free himself from them by the passionate longing for spiritual growth; but it does not, it cannot, give happiness, which is only found when the separate self is cast away and the great Self is recognised as that for the sake of which we are living in the world. Even in ordinary life the unselfish people are the happiest—those who work to make others happy, and who forget themselves. The dissatisfied people are those who are ever seeking happiness for themselves.

We are the Self, and therefore the joys and the sorrows of others are ours as much as theirs, and in proportion as we feel this, and learn to live so that the whole world shares the life that flows through us, do our minds learn the Secret of Peace.

"He attaineth Peace, into whom all desires flow as rivers flow into the ocean, which is filled with water but remaineth unmoved—not he who desireth desire."[1] The more we desire, the more the craving for happiness—which is unhappiness—must grow. The Secret of Peace is the knowledge of the Self, and the thought "That Self am I" will help towards the gaining of a peace of mind that nothing can disturb.

---

[1] *Bhagavad-Gita,* ii. 70.

CHAPTER X

HELPING OTHERS BY THOUGHT

MOST valuable of all the gains made by the worker for thought power, is the increased ability to help those around him, those weaker ones who have not yet learned to utilize their own powers. With his own mind and heart at peace, he is fitted to help others.

A mere kind thought is helpful in its measure, but the student will wish to do far more than drop a mere crumb to the starving.

Let us take first the case of a man who is under the sway of an evil habit, such as drink, and whom a student wishes to help. He should first ascertain, if possible, at what hours the patient's mind is likely to be unemployed—such as his hour for going to bed. If the man should be asleep, it would be all the better. At such a time, he should sit down alone, and picture the image of his patient as vividly as he can, seated in front of him—picture him clearly and in detail, so that he may see the image as he would see the man. (This very clear picturing is not essential, although the process is thereby rendered more effective.) Then he should fix his attention on this image, and address to it, with all the concentration of which he is capable, the thoughts, one by one and slowly, which he wishes to impress on his patient's mind. He should present them as clear mental images, just as he would do if laying arguments before him in words. In the case taken, he might place before him vivid pictures of the disease and misery entailed by the drink-habit, the nervous breakdown, the inevitable end. If the patient is asleep, he will be drawn to the person thus thinking of him, and will animate the image of himself that has been formed. Success depends on the concentration and the steadiness of the thought directed to the patient, and just in proportion to the development of the thought power will be its effect.

Care must be taken in such a case not to try to control, in any way, the patient's will; the effort should be wholly directed towards placing before his mind the ideas which, appealing to his intelligence and emotions, may stimulate him to come to a right judgment and to make an effort to carry it out in action. If an attempt is made to impose on him a particular line of conduct, and the attempt succeed even then little has been gained. The mental tendency towards vicious self-indulgence will not be changed by opposing an obstacle in the way of indulging in a particular form of it; checked in one direction it will find another, and a new vice will supplant the old. A man forcibly constrained to temperance by the domination of his will is no more cured of the vice than if he were locked up in prison. Apart from this, no man should try to impose his will on another, even in order to make him do right. Growth is not helped by such external coercion; the intelligence must be convinced, the emotion aroused and purified, else no real gain is made.

If the student wishes to give any other kind of thought-help, he should proceed in the same way, picturing his friend, and clearly presenting the ideas he wishes to convey. A strong wish for his good, sent to him as a general protective agency, will remain about him as a thought-form for a time proportionate to the strength of the thought, and will guard him against evil, acting as a barrier against hostile thoughts, and even warding off physical dangers. A thought of peace and consolation similarly sent will sooth and calm the mind, spreading around its object an atmosphere of calm.

The aid which is often rendered to another by prayer is largely of the character described above, the frequent effectiveness of prayer over ordinary good wishes being due to the greater concentration and intensity thrown by the pious believer into his prayer. Similar concentration and intensity would bring about similar results without the use of prayer.

There is, of course, another way in which prayer is sometimes effective: it calls the attention of some superhuman, or evolved human, intelligence to the person for whom it is offered, and direct aid may then be rendered to him by a power surpassing that of the offerer of the prayer.

Perhaps it is as well here to interject the remark that the half-instructed should not take alarm and refrain from giving to a friend any thought-assistance of which he is capable, by the fear lest he should be "interfering with karma." Let him leave karma to take care of itself, and have no more fear of interfering with it than of interfering with the law of gravitation. If he can help his friend, let him do so fearlessly, confident in the fact that, if he can do so, that help is within his friend's karma, and that he is himself the happy agent of the Law.

HELPING THE SO-CALLED DEAD

All that we can do for the living by thought we can do even more easily for those who have gone in front of us through death's gateway, for in their case there is no heavy physical matter to be set vibrating ere the thought can reach the waking consciousness.

After death is passed through, the tendency of the man is to turn his attention inwards, and to live in the mind rather than in an external world. The thought-currents that used to rush outwards, seeking the external world through the sense-organs, now find themselves blocked by an emptiness, caused by the disappearance of their instruments. It is as though a man, rushing towards an accustomed bridge over a ravine, suddenly found himself stopped by the bridgeless gulf, the bridge having vanished.

The re-arrangement of the astral body that quickly follows on the loss of the physical body further tends to shut in the mental energies, to prevent their outer expression. The astral matter, if not disturbed by any action of those left behind on earth, forms an enclosing shell instead of a plastic instrument, and the higher and purer the earth-life that has ended, the more complete is the barrier against impressions from without, or emergence from within. But the person thus checked as to his outward-going energies is all the more receptive of influences from the mental world, and he can therefore be helped, cheered, and counselled far more effectively than when he was on earth.

In the world into which those freed from the

physical body have gone, a loving thought is as palpable to the senses as is here a loving word or tender caress. Everyone who passes over should, therefore, be followed by thoughts of love and peace, by aspirations for his swift passage onwards through the valley of death to the bright land beyond. Only too many remain in the intermediate state longer than they otherwise would, because it is their bad karma not to have friends who know how to help them from this side of death. And if people on earth knew how much of comfort and of happiness is experienced by the wayfarers to the heavenly worlds from these truly angelic messengers, these thoughts of love and cheer, if they knew the force they had to strengthen and console, none would be left lonely by those who remain behind. The beloved "dead" have surely a claim on our love and care, and even apart from this how great is the consolation to the heart, bereaved of the presence that gave sunshine to life, to be able still to serve the loved one, and surround him on his way by the guardian angels of thought.

The occultists who founded the great religions were not unmindful of this service due from those left on earth to those who had passed onwards. The Hindu has his Shraddha, by which he helps on their way the souls that have passed into the next world, quickening their passage into Svarga. The Christian Churches have Masses and Prayers for the "dead." "Grant him, O Lord, eternal peace, and let light perpetual shine on him," prays the Christian for his friend in the other world. Only the Protestant section of Christians have lost this gracious custom, with so much else that pertains to the higher life of the Christian man.

THOUGHT-WORK OUT OF THE BODY

We need not confine our thought activities to the hours which we spend in the physical body, for very much effective work may be done by thought when our bodies are lying peacefully asleep.

The process of "going to sleep" is simply the withdrawal of the consciousness, clad in its subtle bodies, from the physical body, which is left wrapped in sleep, while the man himself passes into the astral world. Freed from the physical body, he is much more powerful as regards the effects he can produce by his thought, but for the most part he does not send it outwards, but uses it within himself on subjects that interest him in his waking life. His thought-energies run into accustomed moulds, and work on the problems that his waking consciousness is busy in solving.

The proverb that "the night brings counsel," the advice when an important decision is to be made "to sleep on it before deciding," are vague intuitions of this fact of mental activity during the hours of slumber. Without any deliberate attempt to utilize the freed intelligence, men gather and harvest the fruit of its labour.

Those, however, who seek to steer their evolution instead of allowing it to drift, should consciously avail themselves of the greater powers they can exercise when unimpeded by the weight of the body. The way to do this is simple. Any problem needing solution should be quietly held in the mind when going to sleep; it must not be debated on, argued over, or sleep will be prevented, but, as it were, simply stated and left. This is sufficient to give the required direction to thought, and the Thinker will take it up and deal with it when freed from the physical body. The solution will generally be in the mind on waking, *i.e.*, the Thinker will have impressed it on the brain—and it is a good plan to keep paper and pencil by the bed to note down the solution immediately on waking, as a thought thus obtained is very readily erased by the thronging stimuli from the physical world, and is not easily recovered. Many a difficulty in life may be seen clearly in this way, and a tangled path rendered open. And many a mental problem may also find its solution, when submitted to the intelligence unweighted by the dense brain.

Much in the same way may a student help during the hours of sleep any friend in this world or in the next. He must picture his friend in his mind, and determine to find and help him. That mental image will draw him and his friend together, and they will communicate with each other in the astral world. But in any case in which any emotion is aroused by the thought of the friend—as in the case of one who has passed on—the student must seek to calm it ere going to sleep. For emotion causes a swirl in the astral body, and if that body be in a state of strong agitation, it isolates the consciousness, and makes it impossible for mental vibrations to pass outwards.

In some cases of such communication in the astral world, a "dream" may remain in the waking memory, while in others no trace may appear. The dream is the record—often confused and mixed with alien vibrations—of the meeting out of the body, and should be so regarded. But if no trace appear in the brain, it does not matter, since the activities of the freed intelligence are not hindered by the ignorance of the

brain that does not share them. A man's usefulness
in the astral world is not governed by the memories
imprinted on the brain by the returning consciousness, and these memories may be entirely absent,
while most beneficent work is occupying the hours
of the body's sleep.

Another form of thought-work that is little remembered, and that can be done either in or out of
the physical body, is the helping of good causes, of
public movements beneficial to mankind. To think
of these in a definite way is to start currents of aid
from the inner planes of being, and we may especially
consider this in relation to

THE POWER OF COMBINED THOUGHT

The increased force that may be obtained by the
union of several people to help a common object is
recognized not only by occultists, but by all who
know anything of the deeper science of the mind.
It is the custom, in some parts at least of Christen-
dom, to preface the sending of a mission to evange-
lize some special district by definite and sustained
thinking. A small band of Roman Catholics, for
instance, will meet together for some weeks or months
before a mission is sent out, and will prepare the
ground where it is to work by imaging the place,
thinking of themselves as present there, and then
intently meditating on some definite dogma of the
Church. In this way a thought-atmosphere is created
in that district most favourable to the spread of
Roman Catholic teachings, and receptive brains are
prepared to wish to receive instruction in them.
The thought-work will be aided by the added inten-

sity given to it by fervent prayer, another form of thought-work, fired by religious fervour.

The contemplative orders of the Roman Catholic Church do a large amount of good and useful work by thought, as do the recluses of the Hindu and Buddhist faiths. Wherever a good and pure intelligence sets itself to work to aid the world by diffusing through it noble and lofty thoughts, there definite service is done to man, and the lonely thinker becomes one of the lifters of the world.

AFTERWORD

THUS we may learn to utilize these great forces that lie within us all, and to utilize them to the best possible effect. As we use them they will grow, until, with surprise and delight, we shall find how great a power of service we possess.

Let it be remembered that we are continually using these powers, unconsciously, spasmodically, feebly, affecting ever for good or ill all who surround our path in life. It is here sought to induce the reader to use these same forces consciously, steadily, and strongly. We cannot help thinking to some extent, however weak may be the thought-currents we generate. We *must* affect those around us, whether we will or not; the only question we have to decide is whether we will do it beneficially or mischievously, feebly or strongly, driftingly or of set purpose. We cannot help the thoughts of others touching our minds; we can only choose which we will receive, which reject. We must affect and be affected; but we may affect others for their benefit or their injury, we may be affected by the good or by the evil. Here lies our choice, a choice momentous for ourselves and for the world:

Choose well; for your choice
Is brief and yet endless.

PEACE TO ALL BEINGS

INDEX

A

Quest publishes books on Healing, Health and Diet, Occultism and Mysticism, Philosophy, Transpersonal Psychology, Reincarnation, Religion, The Theosophical Philosophy, Yoga and Meditation. **Other Quest books include:**

The Astral Body by A. E. Powell
An in-depth study of our subtle bodies.

The Atman Project by Ken Wilber
A transpersonal view of human development.

Between Two Worlds by Frederic Wiedemann
Using the soul to integrate personality with spiritual nature.

Beyond the Post-Modern Mind by Huston Smith
A look beyond reductionism and our materialistic culture.

The Chakras by Charles W. Leadbeater
Illustrated examination of energy centers in the body.

Encounter with Awareness by R. Puligandla
Study of pure consciousness that comprises our essential being.

The Etheric Double by A. E. Powell
The health aura. What it is and what it does.

Evolution of Integral Consciousness by H. Chaudhuri
Study of consciousness as a holistic phenomenon.

Expansion of Awareness by A. W. Osborn
One man's search for meaning in life.

Rhythm of Wholeness by Dane Rudhyar
A study of the continuous process of being.

Available from:
The Theosophical Publishing House
306 West Geneva Road, Wheaton, Illinois 60187